Praise for *The Success Guide*

M000191820

Finally, a guide that provides actionable items folks can use to be successful working at home and being their own boss! I've been working remotely now for over two years, and *The Work At Home Success Guide* gave me so many great insights to shift my mindset and continue to grow my business.

— Lauren Gill, Mooring Advisory Group

I don't know a soul who doesn't dream of setting their own schedule, working when they want and where they want. *The Work At Home Success Guide* gives you an inside track to building a successful career while working from home. Freelancers and remote employees alike will discover what it takes to find the best-paying jobs, stay competitive, and create long-term stability in an overcrowded global marketplace.

— Kathryn Rose, CEO wiseHer

As you dive into *The Work At Home Success Guide*, you will feel yourself pulled under the wing of a veteran entrepreneur. The cozy, warm wing of a momma bird who is moments away from booting you out of the nest and into the rest of your life—your dream-chasing life! A good momma bird doesn't just let you stay comfortable, but rather prepares you for what is to come. Julie Eason does exactly that. She doesn't sugarcoat a single thing. She doesn't romanticize or exaggerate stories. She simply gives you what you need to be truly successful working from home.

— Rachel Pedersen, CEO Social Media United, The Viral Touch

I didn't just enjoy it, I smiled the entire way through it. I love how Julie did it and how much she "gets it." This book needs to be in the hands of anyone who has ever thought for one second that they might want to work from home. And they should have their pencil and highlighter ready to mark the numerous ideas and strategic details throughout the book that they'll want to revisit over and over again. There was so much fantastic content that any business professional could find valuable, and effective takeaways to help them be more successful.

From ideation to overcoming obstacles, strategic thinking, practical planning, marketing, relationship selling, resources and solutions—it was like easy access to an excellent mentor on every page. This is more than a brilliant success guide full of creative ideas, strategic solutions, valuable resources, and effective marketing tips. This is a work-from-home mentor disguised as a book for practical tips and details to consider at every stage from ideation through execution.

— Christy Long Hoskins, CEO Professionalpedia

The Work At Home Success Guide is THE must-have, step-by-step manual for anyone considering a career without a commute. A highly enjoyable read, this book is packed with solid gold, practical advice from an industry expert on every possible aspect of working from home. A work-from-home veteran myself, I hadn't expected I'd be taking quite so many notes! It's excellent.

— Lisa Cherry Beaumont, author of *Life Purpose Alchemy: Discover What Fulfils You and Do What You Love for a Living*

The
WORK At HOME
SUCCESS
GUIDE

How To Make More Money
with Freelance, Telecommuting,
and Remote Working Jobs

by
Julie Anne Eason

Print ISBN: 978-1-944602-19-2

Thanet House Publishing, LLC
848 N. Rainbow Blvd. #750
Las Vegas, NV 89107

DISCLAIMER: This is a work of non-fiction. The information is of a general nature to help you on the subject of freelance and remote working. Readers of this publication agree that the author and Thanet House Publishing will not be held responsible or liable for damages that may be alleged or resulting directly or indirectly from their use of this publication. All external links are provided as a resource only and are not guaranteed to remain active for any length of time. The author cannot be held accountable for the information provided by, or actions resulting from, accessing these resources.

Publisher's Cataloging-In-Publication Data
(Prepared by The Donohue Group, Inc.)

Names: Eason, Julie Anne, author.
Title: The work at home success guide : how to make more money with freelance, telecommuting, and remote working jobs / by Julie Anne Eason.
Description: Las Vegas, NV : Thanet House Books, [2018] | Includes bibliographical references.
Identifiers: ISBN 9781944602192 (print) | ISBN 9781944602208 (ebook)
Subjects: LCSH: Telecommuting. | Home-based businesses. | Self-employed. | Success in business.
Classification: LCC HD2336.3 .E27 2018 (print) | LCC HD2336.3 (ebook) | DDC 658.3/123--dc23

Edited by Julia Willson
Interior and Ebook layout by Soumi Goswami

Dedication

For my mother, Catherine.
Thank you for teaching me that I could
be whoever and whatever I want to be.
You gave me the tools to chart my own course.
I am forever grateful.

Contents

Foreword

I'll never forget the day I met Julie. I mean…how could I? If you've met her, you know exactly what I'm talking about. If you haven't had that good fortune, be ready to experience how her words and voice imprint deeply on your soul as you read.

I've met and worked with a lot of entrepreneurs over the years. Yet there aren't many people whose opinions and expertise I rely on. Julie is one of the few people I truly listen to. She has more than 20 years of writing experience, several best-selling books, and a decade of entrepreneurship (read: experience) under her belt.

While I still consider myself a baby entrepreneur, I lead a community of over 20,000 entrepreneurs who work from home, so I know the remote working world and which way is up. And I'm so thrilled that you're holding this book in your hands.

As you dive into *The Work At Home Success Guide*, you will feel yourself pulled under the wing of a veteran entrepreneur. The cozy, warm wing of a momma-bird businesswoman who is moments away from booting you out of the nest and into the rest of your life—your dream-chasing life. A good momma bird doesn't just let you stay comfortable, but rather prepares you for what is to come. Julie does exactly that.

Entrepreneurship can be one of the most terrifying and rewarding experiences. As a mother of three young children and founder/CEO of two businesses, I often look to leaders who have blazed the trail of success, balance (or embracing the lack thereof at times), and grit. I watch their lives closely to see if their words and actions match up.

What I love about Julie is that she will never sugarcoat a single thing. She also doesn't romanticize or exaggerate stories. Do not mistake her storytelling abilities for fantasy—this book is nonfiction to its core.

No matter where you are on your journey—just starting or already years into the remote-working adventure—you're in for a treat. It's time for me to be quiet and allow you to fall in love with this book.

Rachel Pedersen
CEO, Social Media United, The Viral Touch

Whatever you want to do—do it.
Whatever you want to be—be it.
The resources exist.
The time is now.
I believe in you.

Introduction

Celia's heart beat faster as she made her way to the boss's office. Her throat tightened. What could they possibly find wrong now? *Just breathe*, she thought. *It's almost Friday.*

Sam sipped his lukewarm coffee and stared out the cafeteria window at the bright sunshine. It was only 10:00 a.m. It would be seven more mind-numbing hours before he could go outside and breathe some fresh air. Maybe there would be enough daylight left to go for a quick bike ride with the kids. *It's almost Friday*, he thought.

Little beads of nervous sweat broke out on Elizabeth's forehead as she swiped her debit card. Had the rent check cleared yet? If she didn't find work soon…

Scenes like this play out every day for millions of people all over the world. They're stuck in jobs they hate or that bore them to death. Or they've been downsized, laid off—those unemployment benefits don't last forever.

Some of these people are moms and dads who've spent the past 10 years raising children, and now have no idea how to get back into the workforce. They just want the freedom to attend their kids' softball games and school plays. Those who are employed often deal with some sort of workplace drama on a daily basis. Bosses screaming at them, coworkers blaming each other, pointless meetings, bullying, and office gossip.

The old work paradigm is clearly broken.

There's a joy crisis in the modern world, and it's crushing our collective soul.

In the US, adults are expected to spend 40 hours or more every week doing something that earns a paycheck. The hours we work January through May make just enough money to pay taxes for the year, and we're often allowed only a few days off. Extended breaks are rare.

As children, we are taught that the best way to get ahead is to earn good grades in school, attend a good college, and get a good job. If we do that, we'll be set up for a good life. That might have been possible a few generations ago, but these days, going to a "respectable" college often means a lifetime of debt, and working your tail off for a company that may or may not provide security.

Businesses restructure every day. Jobs come and go. Technology moves so fast that entire industries can dry up overnight, leaving people wondering, "How am I going to survive? How will I provide for my family?"

The most important skill a person can have in the twenty-first century is self-reliance. That means when the traditional employment model doesn't work, you know that you can create your own job. When the office environment is simply soul-crushing, you know there's another way. The technology exists. So many jobs these days can be undertaken at home. Or at a ball game. Or in another country. There are thousands of jobs that can be performed anywhere.

There's no need to work for a boss you despise.

There's no need to put up with office bullies.

You don't have to suffer through nine hours of work, if you can complete the day's tasks in two.

And you don't have to give up caring for your family just to collect a paycheck.

Millions of people are stuck in their current jobs, wishing they could work from home doing something they love. Millions more are stuck at home wishing they had jobs at all.

The solution for both groups is working ANYWHERE, ANYWHEN. You're going to see the different ways of achieving "work-from-home" status starting in the very next chapter. But whether you call it telecommuting, entrepreneurship, remote working, or freelancing, you have skills that other people need. You can provide those skills as a service and set up your own rules for how you'll work.

Want to work from home? You can. Want to travel? Groovy! Want to work two days a week and go surfing the other five? It's possible.

When you adopt the anywhere, anywhen mindset, you're the boss. You decide where you work. You decide when you work. You decide how much you'll work. And even how much you charge.

The meaning of "work" is shifting. Actually, it has already shifted. According to the U.S. Government Accountability Office and the Bureau of Labor Statistics, over 40% of the entire American workforce does not clock in at an office or work the standard 40-hour week anymore. Those people are part of a new classification of workers called "contingent."

Employers are discovering that not only can they get better productivity from remote workers, they also save money on overhead costs. They don't have to provide offices, pay for electricity, or upgrade computers every year. And their employees are actually happier. When companies hire freelancers or independent contractors, they don't have to pay for benefits such as health insurance or payroll taxes.

Remote workers are finding that they can get much more accomplished in less time and they can earn more money. And they no longer have to deal with a commute or office politics. And often that alone is more than enough to offset the lack of company benefits.

Work where you want, when you want, and make as much as you want. Sounds great, right?

It is! I've been running my own freelance writing business for nearly 30 years now, and I couldn't return to traditional employment if I wanted to. I have no patience for inefficiency or mean-spirited people. I've carved out a life I love and made my own rules along the way.

It hasn't always been easy. When I started, there was no email or internet. I had to send stories to magazines in the mail, with stamps and everything. But today, I run my entire business from a laptop.

How Did I Get Here?

A sharp, searing pain started in my lower back, then wrapped its red-hot fingers around my belly and squeezed. It would let up for a little while, then I could feel the tension build and it would happen all over again. For 23 hours straight.

It's funny how people compare starting a business to giving birth. What starts as pain and blood, sweat, and tears eventually gives way to a feeling of euphoria and love (thanks to those postpartum hormones). Soon after that, the sleep deprivation period starts and you'd give anything for just a few hours of alone time.

When my own labor pains subsided, I knew I wanted nothing more than to stay home and raise my beautiful daughter. I wanted to be there for every moment—her first words, her first steps, her first heartbreak. Becoming a stay-at-home mom just felt right. It was what I was supposed to do. Thank heaven I have an amazingly supportive husband who wanted that stable influence for his daughter as much as I did. He had a good job and provided the much-needed regular paycheck.

As our family grew (we eventually had three children), I began to experience what I can only describe as mom guilt. As hard as I was working at home raising the kids, I had this gnawing feeling in my gut that I should be doing more, contributing more, bringing in at least a small income to help out. My husband never complained or even hinted that I needed to do more. But that didn't stop me from feeling that if I could just bring in $100 a month, our lives would change. After all, $100 could buy a lot of diapers back then.

I also experienced something I call mom boredom. Raising kids is extremely rewarding; it's also tedious at times. There were days I didn't talk to another adult for 8 to 10 hours at a time. As an extrovert, I found that draining. I craved conversation and interaction. We lived in rural Maine, so it wasn't as if there were playgroups on every block. And this was pre-internet, so there were no online forums or blogs or communities to participate in. It was me and the kids most of the time. (I now completely understand why I talk to myself—out loud—regularly.)

So, I tried to figure out what I could do that would bring in a small income and give me some mental stimulation. I had been writing stories my whole life. Writing came easy for me, and I truly enjoyed it. So, I figured I'd be a writer. I would write novels while the kids slept, and everything would be magical. Stephen King lived just up the road. If he could do it, so could I.

I quickly learned that writing a novel suitable for publication takes a really long time. It could be years before I saw a penny of profit, and that was IF my book was any good. (I later found out from an agent that it was "okay" but my fiction needed a lot of work to be a source of income.)

But it wasn't the stories I loved so much as the process of writing. It was amazing to me that I could create something valuable from merely recording my thoughts. So, I searched for other ways to make money by writing.

By sheer luck, I ran across a book called *The Well-Fed Writer* by Peter Bowerman. Inside that book, he described all sorts of ways to make money through writing. You could write brochures, white papers, annual reports, booklets, advertising slogans—the list went on and on.

I also learned that the glossy magazines I read every month paid freelancers to write articles. And radio stations paid writers to create their clients' ads. And on and on. My imagination soared! Business people needed writing. I could write. It was a match made in heaven.

Just on a whim, I approached our tiny local newspaper to see if they needed anyone to write anything. It turned out they needed someone to cover the local school board and municipal meetings. All I had to do was attend the meetings and write up a short article about what was discussed. They paid $25 a meeting, and there were usually four meetings a month. Sweet! How easy can you get? I had my $100 a month, and all I had to do was report on what people said. The meetings were at night, so I didn't even have to hire a sitter for the kids.

That early job wasn't everything I'd hoped it would be. If you've never attended a board of selectmen's meeting in a rural New England town, let me enlighten you. The meetings were boring, the rooms were overheated, and it was usually just three guys and me. So, I couldn't exactly nod off in the corner unnoticed. Occasionally, there would be something interesting going on. But usually I had to get really creative to write 250 words about the potholes that needed filling on Wilbur's Farm Road.

Still, those $100 checks helped us out. A lot. And I felt a sense of satisfaction that something I wrote was worth money.

Eventually, I did start writing for those glossy magazines, and many other businesses, both locally and around the world. It's been over 25 years now, my kids are grown, and I am thrilled that it won't be long before my husband retires and we can live off my earnings for the rest of our lives. Over the past two decades, I've been a journalist, a copywriter, a content writer, and a ghostwriter. I've been paid to write two-sentence ads, and I've been paid to write full-length books—including *Wall Street Journal* and *New York Times* bestsellers!

Writing has given me the freedom to raise my family on my own terms and the self-satisfaction of contributing financially. The best part was that I could write from any place I wanted. I could write anytime I wanted. There were no rules. No boss was breathing down my neck with unreasonable demands. And while sometimes the subjects were a bit dry, I was never bored.

There were plenty of times I cried behind my bedroom door, wondering what the heck I was doing. Where were the new clients? How could I get more money for the work I was doing? Was I good enough to write for a big company? Was I dreaming to think I could write a whole book? But it didn't matter how nervous I was, I wanted the work. So, I learned that if a client asks you whether you can do something, you should always say, "Yes!" And then you go figure out how to make it happen. Even if you really aren't sure you can handle it, you still say yes.

I've been blessed. I've made a ton of mistakes and learned a lot of lessons. And I want to scream from the rooftops, "YOU CAN DO IT, TOO!"

As I mentioned, back when I was starting out, there was no internet, no email. I didn't even have a computer for a long time. I typed out my stories and mailed them in hand-addressed, stamped envelopes. Then I had to wait for the checks to be cut and mailed. I developed a love/hate relationship with my mailbox. Sometimes there was a check, sometimes a rejection letter. (But it was at the end of a long driveway, so at least I got some exercise.)

Technology has evolved to the point where just about anyone can work this way. In fact, a huge percentage of workers already do. The world of offices and teams that meet face-to-face every day are becoming obsolete. We all want the freedom to do our work on our own time. We all want to watch our kids play soccer and to attend their dance recitals. We all want to take vacations whenever we want. And we all want the ability to set our own salaries.

You want to make more money? You can! When you work on a freelance basis, there's no artificial ceiling for how much you can earn. And even when you work remotely for one employer, you can still decide to start a second business on your own time.

You want to be truly prepared for retirement? Spend some of your time creating passive income streams that pay you whether you work or not.

You want to guarantee you'll never be laid off? Become your own boss. That's the only real security.

Tired of office politics? Get out of the office!

The opportunities are out there. And not just for writers. If you can do graphic design…or code a website…or type…or answer the phone—there's a remote work option for you. Still paying off loans from medical school? Even high-level professionals are finding ways to work outside an office environment.

Tele-radiologist—that's a job! So are tele-nurse and tele-pharmacist.

Really?

Really!

If there isn't a job for your skill set and interests already, you can invent one.

And if you're currently in an employment emergency—and you need cash RIGHT NOW—working anywhere, anywhen is one of the fastest ways to dig yourself out of the hole you're in and get back on the road to success.

I've unofficially coached people to step out on their own for my entire career. When they find out what I do, they ask questions. And I want to help them. It's gotten so common for me to receive emails about freelancing that I decided it was time to write a book about it. Because there are challenges. People aren't trained how to land clients or collect invoices. They're taught how to write résumés. They spend 12 years in school learning how to sit still for 8 hours and just do the work. Someone else's work. For someone else's profit. By someone else's rules.

You will need to develop new skills, adopt different mindsets, and completely redefine what it means to "work." Once you do, you'll find some amazing opportunities if you are daring enough to leave traditional work behind.

PLEASE NOTE: If you are currently employed in a traditional job—especially if you have a family to care for—read this entire book and educate yourself before you make the leap. I am NOT suggesting that you quit your job immediately and try to figure everything out as you go. Many people spend way too long trying to get the courage to leave their "secure" jobs, but some others quit too soon. It can take some time to build up a client list or find the right remote work situation, so don't rush it. You got this!

I wrote this book to answer the questions I receive all the time, like...

- How do I set up a business?
- Where do I find clients?
- How much should I charge?
- How do I handle unhappy clients?
- What if I want to be a remote employee instead of a business owner? Where are those jobs?

If you're currently stuck in a job you hate, or you're just starting out, this book will teach you how to ramp up quickly and overcome the obstacles that kept me stuck for years.

If you're already a freelancer or entrepreneur, you'll learn how to make more money and enjoy your success more. You'll learn some ways to increase your income without working additional hours. And you might discover some blind spots you didn't know were keeping you from becoming as successful as you could be.

Yeah, But ...

If you think working anywhere, anywhen is just a dream—something other people do, but it's not for you—allow me to dispel a few common myths.

Work-at-home jobs are a scam. Okay, you've got me. Some advertised work-at-home jobs are, indeed, scams. Others ask for money in return for training or a "starter pack" or some other kind of setup materials. Many ads will promise riches if you learn their secret system. You'll find ads for these scams all over the internet, even on legitimate job-search sites. Those are NOT what I'm talking about in this book. I'm talking about real jobs, real careers, working for real companies that need your skills and expertise. Careers such as writing, design, translation, radiology, nursing, engineering, transcription, customer service, sales, and so much more.

Make no mistake—if you're desperately looking for new opportunities, it's easy to fall victim to the scams. So, I want you to do it right. I want you to set yourself up in a situation that makes you happy and makes you money.

But I need a regular paycheck, and my current job is secure. Is it? Is it really secure? Do you know what's going on at the higher levels of the company? There was a time, say 50 years ago, that you could start at the bottom and work your way up the company ladder. You might have stayed with the same company your whole life. That is rarely the case anymore.

The average worker today will change jobs 11 times! Businesses close, companies merge, industries become obsolete, and layoffs can happen out of the blue for just about any reason. If you're happy working for your company, and you feel secure there, great. Congratulations on beating the odds! May you have a long and lucrative career. But if you're reading this book, chances are pretty good you don't feel secure or happy. So, why cling to it? Why not explore some alternatives?

As for that regular paycheck, is it enough? When's the next time you can expect a raise? What's the pay ceiling on your position? Will you need to go back to school or complete further training to climb up the ladder?

A good friend and client of mine likes to say, "Your raise becomes effective when you do." Why settle for what someone else thinks you're worth? Read through this book and you'll discover there are so many opportunities. The world is wide open.

I don't have enough money saved to quit my current job. So don't. Use your creativity to make the transition slowly. Maybe start your freelance business on the side. Anywhere, anywhen—remember? That means you can work for clients on the weekends or your days off. Maybe you can set up an arrangement to go part-time at your current job.

Or what if your boss is open to renegotiating your current contract so you could work from home? Lots of companies are finding they save money and have happier employees when they set up this arrangement. You'll never know if you don't ask. Anywhere, anywhen is all about the possible. What's possible? How can you make it work? How can you earn the money you need AND be happy at the same time?

I need the benefits. Cool. Time to do some math. What benefits do you actually get? And how can you provide those or better for yourself? Health insurance? Systems are set up to help you buy your own. You will have to figure out how much you need to earn to do that, but it might not be as much as you thought. Retirement? When you work anywhere, anywhen, you have more control over the investment vehicles you use to fund your retirement. Maybe real estate is a better deal for you than a 401k. Investing is complicated, but again, there are resources out there to help you.

Paid time off? Hmm, how much is that actually worth? You could work when you want, and take as much time off as you want, without asking for permission and fighting with coworkers for the most popular weeks. Want to work over the holidays? Cool! Want to take a three-month trip around the world? You can do that. The simpler you live, the less money you need to survive. I don't know about you, but I'd rather decide how to spend my time than have someone else dictate what I can and can't do.

I don't have a degree, certification, or experience. There aren't any jobs out there for me. You have skills. I guarantee you do. Or, at the very least, you can learn some skills. Yes, prior experience can help. If you're a graphic designer with a great portfolio, finding clients might be a little easier. But there are ways to get the experience you need and get paid for it. And unlike a traditional job, you don't need to slave away for years at a low wage. Your skill, confidence, and ability to sell are what determine how much you make—not an expensive piece of paper. In fact, in the first section of this book, I'll help you determine what you're good at, what you might like to learn, and how to apply that to make money.

I don't like to sell. If you're going to work for clients, you will have to do some selling. Later on, I'll show you how to have a simple sales conversation that has clients ready to work with you without any hard sales tactics. But you don't have to work with clients. You can still work remotely while employed by a company. There are hundreds of thousands of jobs you can apply for all over the world. I'll show you where to find them and how to land them.

What if I fail? Hmm. But what if you don't? What if you become wildly successful and enjoy a quality of life you never dreamed you could have? It's true, you might fail. But the beauty of working remotely is that you can pick yourself right back up and try again. There are always more clients. There are always new skills you can learn. If you get bored with one type of job, you can transition to another.

Temporary failure is inevitable, no matter what kind of job you have. When you're the boss, though, you can decide whether to beat yourself up over the failure, or whether to chalk it up as a learning experience and move on.

Confidence and positive mindset are huge contributors to success in this type of career. And it takes time to develop strong confidence levels. But it's easier and faster to build those muscles when you don't have a nasty commute or unpleasant coworkers tearing you down. Toward the end of the book, you'll find several strategies for building your confidence and resilience.

If You're Working Remotely Already, It's Time to Level Up

Considering that such a huge percentage of the workforce around the world is considered nontraditional—freelancers, remote workers, telecommuters, and entrepreneurs—there's a chance you're already working this way. Woo-hoo! Way to go.

But tell me something: Are you making the kind of money you'd like to make? Do you actually take time off? How's your health? No matter how successful you are, there's always room to grow. Even seasoned remote workers can learn from each other and raise their success to the next level.

This book is full of strategies, some of which you might have never heard before. More importantly, you might have some strategies or tools I've never heard before. And I'm always up for a new idea.

You've Got This!

Working anywhere, anywhen isn't just for lucky people. It's not just for people with tons of experience or big savings accounts. It's not even particularly competitive when you have the right strategies and mindset. Anyone can do this. YOU can do this. The technology is out there. The training is free, in many cases. And you can learn as you go. If you're tired of your work environment, or you're unemployed and discouraged by the traditional job market, let this book open your eyes to what's possible.

You can do it.

I believe in you.

Let's get started!

SECTION 1:

GETTING READY

Decide

People waffle all the time. They sit in their cubicles dreaming of "someday."

"If only…" becomes their mantra.

If only they could save enough money. If only they could pay off the house. If only it wasn't so expensive to live in this city. It's like a drug, that "if only" statement. It allows us a moment or two of hope. We get to fantasize about the world we want before we come back down to reality.

What's your drug of choice? Do you find yourself repeating the same phrase over and over followed by whatever condition must be perfect before you can take charge of your life?

If only…

As soon as…

I wish…

It must be nice to…

Someday…

Making that decision is the first step to freedom. Deciding to be your own boss. Deciding where and when you will work. Deciding what kind of work you will do. Deciding that freedom of choice is more valuable than the perceived security of a 9–5 job. Sometimes that decision is scary. Sometimes it takes everything you have just to admit to yourself that you want it. But decisions hold tremendous power. They open the doors to possibilities.

Once you decide you're going to take charge of your own work, the phrases change from wishful dreaming to the beginnings of plans.

> *If only* becomes **What if…**
>
> *As soon as* becomes **When…**
>
> *I wish…* becomes **I will…**
>
> *It must be nice to* becomes **It will be nice when…**
>
> *Someday* becomes **Someday soon…**

That's all you need to begin your journey. That simple shift in thinking from *if only* to **what if** can work magic in your brain. You may have no idea what you want to do. You may not see any way out of your current working situation. You may be working at home already, and fearful that you'll never make enough money to survive. You may be unemployed or disabled or just graduating from school.

That's okay.

Make the shift in your thinking.

Decide that success will be yours.

…

…

…

Have you decided? Great!

Now what?

Well, that's up to you. There are people who up and quit their 9–5 cold turkey and do just fine. Most of the time, though, they struggle a bit first. Some of them struggle a lot. You might not be that kind of adrenaline seeker who's ready to jump off the employment cliff and grow wings on the way down. And that's okay…as long as you don't use your desire for security as an excuse to keep you trapped.

Other people wait until that magical someday when they've saved enough money to live comfortably for a certain amount of time—three months, six months, a year. While it's certainly a good idea to have money put away, sometimes that time cushion can actually hinder your success. It's easy to fall into the trap of underachieving just because you have money put away. It's almost like some people don't really take their new situation seriously until they run out of savings. Scary! You want to hit the ground running, ready to start getting those paying gigs as soon as possible. It might help to think of your savings as an emergency fund, rather than your "ramping up" money.

There are a few ways you can start to move toward working at home full-time even without major savings. The first way happens to so many people—they get laid off. They "become redundant," as they say in the UK. That pink slip comes one day, and that's it. It's not much fun, but this symbolic piece of paper is a totally valid way to start your new endeavor. Considering that layoffs can sneak up on you out of the blue, it's probably a good idea to have some sort of work-at-home backup plan anyway, don't you think?

Okay, let's assume you're not about to get laid off. What's the plan?

If you're already employed, you can simply continue that job and start working a "side hustle" during your spare time. Yes, that means you're essentially working two jobs. And that's okay for a little while. One of the biggest benefits of working at home is that you get to decide when you work. So, for the time being, decide you're going to work the side hustle before your 9–5. Or after. Or on your lunch break. Or on the weekends.

If your goal is to quit your current job completely, then don't dabble at your side gig. Treat it with as much or more intensity as your 9–5. Work it harder. Work it smarter. Get good at it as quickly as you can. It's going to take work, especially at the beginning. You'll be working long hours, and you might even second-guess your decision. Be prepared for it and embrace the journey.

If you're working it right and you have a little luck on your side, that side gig will become busier than your regular job, and you'll have to make a choice. You might decide that the free-lance thing wasn't as great as you thought it would be, and you just drop it and go back to your 9–5 exclusively. More likely, though, it's time to ditch that steady paycheck and run headlong into your new adventure.

Please realize you don't have to quit your job all at once! Quite often, you can simply reduce your hours to part-time. Or you might even be able to do your regular job from home, if you just talk to your boss honestly about your desire for a differ-ent working environment. All sorts of solutions can be worked out with some honesty and good communication.

Some people commit to their dream gig 100%, then choose a sort-of-steady paycheck as their side gig. Maybe they are reg-istered with a temp agency and work in an office a few days a week. Or maybe they sign up as a substitute teacher at a local school. (In many places, you don't need an education back-ground to be a substitute.) Maybe you get a weekend job at the mall while you work to fill your client roster during the week. However you manage to make ends meet while you're getting started is perfect. (You know, assuming it's legal…)

Fast or slow, your transition is entirely up to you. There are so many ways to quit your daily office grind. You can take baby steps or one giant leap. You don't have to know everything or have it all figured out ahead of time. Listen to your intuition and create the right path for you. It all starts with a decision.

Career Design in Three Steps

Are you dreaming about the freedom, but not sure what kind of work you could be doing? You're not alone. So many people tell themselves remote working is impossible because of the kind of job they're currently doing.

Here's the deal: What you do now does not have to be forever. You can reinvent yourself. You can start over. It might mean a pay cut…then again, it might not. And if you're just beginning your career journey, you can choose to work anywhere, anywhen right from the start.

You work to make money, right? Okay, yes, you want to contribute to society and help make the world a better place. But you also need a paycheck. So, let's break this down into really simple steps. You make money by helping people. The more people you help, the more money you make. Are you with me so far?

All you have to do to earn money and have the lifestyle you want is figure out how you can help lots of people by doing something you love. Maybe you're already doing that work, you just need to find more people to help or to adjust your lifestyle requirements. Maybe you need to scrap what you're doing and start over. And just so we're clear, you don't have to have a burning passion for what you choose to do. There will probably be parts of the job you don't enjoy. But if you're going to design your career, why not choose something you like?

When I was growing up, I never really thought about what job I wanted to have. I had vague dreams of becoming either an astronaut or a ballerina, but I never truly believed either of those was possible. I didn't plan out what kind of lifestyle I wanted, or what kind of work I wanted to do. I never said, "I want to be a writer when I grow up." That career just sort of happened to me while I was busy being a mom.

The world is a completely different place now. It's not only possible but fairly easy to design your career to fit the way you want to live. And if your desires change over time, you can redesign your career just as easily. Technology connects us to the whole world. We have billions of potential clients and customers. With the right mindset and skills, you can make a career out of just about anything. Designing work that fits into the anywhere, anywhen model can be accomplished in three simple steps.

Step 1: WHAT

The first step is deciding what you want to do. I stumbled into my writing career because I knew I could write. It's something I'd done for fun since childhood. When the chance came along to get paid to write an article, I did it, just because I could. When you're figuring out what you might like to do, it could be helpful to explore these questions.

- What *can* I do?
- What do I *like* to do?
- What would I like to *learn* how to do?

It's helpful to make a three-column list using these questions as the headers. Then look across them and see if there are similarities.

- If you can write and you enjoy watching movies, maybe you could be a movie reviewer or a screenwriter.

- If you can talk on the phone and you enjoy solving problems, maybe you'd make a great customer service representative.
- If you can understand large lists of data and you enjoy chemistry, maybe a tele-pharmacy job is in your future.

Remember, you can always learn new skills if necessary. Some kinds of training will take longer than others. For example, a movie critic won't need as much schooling as a pharmacist. Think outside the traditional career box. If you like to do something unusual, write it down. You could invent a completely new job!

A gentleman named Jacob Hiller wanted more than anything to be able to dunk a basketball when he was little. So, he learned how to jump. He spent years learning all the different ways to jump higher. Then he started a YouTube channel documenting what he learned and teaching others how to jump. Then he wrote a book about it, *The Jump Manual*. Today, he travels around the world jumping with different groups of people. Seriously. He became a highly successful expert at increasing people's vertical jumps. That's his business—jumping. Not exactly a traditional career choice! And certainly not something most kids dream of doing when they grow up.

Another gentleman grew up with a fascination for big tires. He loved any giant machine—tractors, cranes, earth-movers of all kinds. And he especially loved the tires. Sounds weird, right? Well, today he is probably the world's only big-tire expert. Companies pay him considerable consultation fees to travel around the world making sure those giant machines have the safest, most appropriate tires to keep their employees and cargo safe. Sounds pretty cool, huh?

Spend some time brainstorming and dreaming for a while. How could you make a career out of what you love?

A friend of mine loves sewing historical costumes. She's written a book on Victorian clothing, and she has a home-based career creating mannequins for museum exhibits. Another friend loves iPhone apps, and built a business helping other people create their own apps. There are people who get paid to play video games and find the glitches. What do you love?

Step 2: WHO

Once you know what you might like to do, the next step is figuring out who needs that done. Who might hire you, either as an employee, freelancer, or consultant? Or if you're creating something for sale, who might want to buy what you're creating? It doesn't matter if you're a fine artist or manufacturer—you've got to find buyers. Otherwise, you don't have a career, you have a hobby.

Again, think outside the traditional box here. If you like to clean up messes and restore order out of chaos, maybe you could be a personal organizer for people's homes. Or you could organize businesses and keep them running smoothly by becoming a project manager.

There are business-to-consumer (B2C) jobs where you provide products and services to the end users. And there are business-to-business (B2B) jobs where you are providing products and services to other businesses. Those other businesses might resell what you sell them, or they might use what you sell them to create their own products. In order to think creatively about your market, ask yourself: *Who in the private sector might buy what I do? And who in the corporate/business world might buy what I do? What kinds of companies might use what I do to create something else?*

Sometimes there are many markets for what you want to do. As a freelance writer, I wrote for magazines and newspapers. I also wrote websites, articles, and books for businesses. Many writers specialize even further into industry niches like banking, medical, fitness, and manufacturing. Specializing makes it easier to pick up new clients. They tend to trust you more if you've already written on similar topics. If you're leaving a job in the banking industry, you might want to stick with that niche while you're ramping up and getting your first freelance clients. Even if you eventually want to shift focus, those early successes will boost your confidence and help keep cash flow steady. It can also be easier to find remote employment if you stick with an industry you're familiar with.

Once you have a skill and a market identified, your next step is to start contacting potential clients or employers.

Step 3: HOW

The final step is figuring out how to reach your market, the people who will buy what you're selling. As you'll learn in upcoming chapters, it's best to start with the low-hanging fruit first. Who do you already know in your market? Do you currently work for a company that might hire you on a freelance basis? Does your best friend have a client who could use what you do? By starting close to home, you'll get those first few buyers faster. That will boost your confidence for later when it's time to start contacting strangers.

Next, broaden your circle to your local town, region, or state. Where do your future clients hang out? And how can you let them know about what you do? This is marketing, and it's an essential skill. Would it be worthwhile to hang flyers up at your local bookstore or supermarket? How can you get your new business mentioned on the radio or local TV? Would the local newspaper be interested in something you have to say? You could start a weekly column, with a byline that tells readers what you do.

Where does your target market hang out online? Are there specific websites or social media groups where you're likely to find lots of buyers? Chances are you already know where to find people, it's just a matter of getting the word out. I'll talk a lot more about how to do that in the upcoming chapters.

TAKE ACTION

Take some time to design your ideal career or job. Write down the answers to the questions in Steps 1–3 and start creating an action plan. If you are already working anywhere, anywhen, take some time to answer the questions anyway. You might uncover new markets to sell your products or services to. Or you might figure out a brand new market for your existing skills.

Freelancer or Remote Employee?

There are two basic types of work-at-home careers. You can be a remote employee or a freelancer/entrepreneur. The difference is your source of income.

A **remote employee** works for one company. They have a boss or manager, a regular paycheck, equipment, support, and possibly benefits from that company. It's just like having a traditional job, but the work is done from home. According to Global Workplace Analytics, telecommuting has increased 103% since 2005. As of 2016, 3.7 million employees worked from home at least part-time.

This can be a wonderful setup if you enjoy the security of a regular paycheck. You can work from just about anywhere, depending on your tech needs. But you'll probably still have vacation and sick time approved by someone else. You'll only be allowed so much paid time off, and you may incur penalties or even corrective action for taking too much time.

Companies large and small are seeing the advantages of this arrangement, and are quickly converting their current onsite staff to remote working environments. They typically reduce their operating costs significantly *and* have happier employees at the same time. Global Workplace Analytics estimates that a typical business can save $11,000 per person per year, even if just a portion of their staff works remotely just half the time. It's a win-win for everyone!

Some companies are making the switch incrementally, testing the waters with a remote-working day once a week. Others are jumping in and converting their entire business to the remote model. Make no mistake, though—I predict remote is the way most work will be done in the future. The younger generations expect it. They know it's possible and don't have any intentions of wasting significant portions of their lives in a daily commute.

Companies also know that with the remote work model, they have access to a global talent pool. They are no longer tied down to people who are physically living in the same location. Sometimes the most talented workers are in a completely different part of the country, or on the other side of the world.

That's great news for employees, too. Suddenly, they don't have to live in the city if they don't want to. They don't even have to live in one place. Depending on the type of work, they can pack up their belongings and travel the world. They can settle down on a farm, hundreds of miles from the nearest major corporation. Or they can chase the summer, always living where it's warm.

We are currently in a transition period. Many executives in charge of making decisions for a company don't always get it. They cling to the old notions of work, believing the only way things get done is through face-to-face meetings and office interactions. Or perhaps they don't understand how employees can be monitored effectively when they are out of sight, ensuring standards of productivity and quality. But those older, outdated ideas are being replaced by younger generations of workers who desire and value freedom, family, and fun. They don't define their worth based on their jobs. They see money as a means to enjoy their lives, and they're not settling for the same old tired routine.

If you're dreaming of a world where you can work where you want, when you want, make it happen! Opportunities are everywhere. Right now. All you have to do is decide that you want it, and go get it. And that's what this book will help you do.

The Gig Economy

Companies are not only reducing costs by getting rid of office spaces, some are also doing away with entire departments. Outsourcing tasks to qualified freelancers or outside agencies is becoming more and more common. So, it only makes sense that the ranks of freelancers are growing, too. In fact, the Freelancer's Union estimated that 53 million Americans considered themselves freelancers in 2014. That's 34% of the entire workforce. And that number continues to grow.

The term "gig economy" has been used to describe this phenomenon. Rather than focusing on getting a job, many people are opting to work a gig that is more short-term. It might be a task completed in a few hours, or it might be a longer-term project that seems like a "real job" to outsiders.

The difference is in how the worker views what they do. Are they invested in a particular company? Do they plan to stay with that one employer and move up the ladder? Or do they consider it just temporary work, an opportunity that they're happy with for now, but one they could happily trade for another job at any time.

In contrast to remote workers, **freelancers** work for a variety of clients. They collect service fees rather than paychecks. They provide their own healthcare, equipment, supplies, training, and anything else they need. In return for that, they get to decide exactly when, where, and how they will work.

If they don't like a particular client, they can opt not to take that job. If they want to spend six months traveling, they can. Freelancing can seem more glamorous than being a remote employee. But you really must pay close attention to your needs.

A freelancer must be both the worker and the marketing department. They must attract the clients, sell the clients, and then complete the work. It can be exhausting, and many freelancers struggle to maintain an even cash flow, especially in the beginning. When you're starting out as a freelancer, it's almost more important to study marketing and sales than it is to perfect your craft. It doesn't matter how great you are at what you do—if you can't get people to hire you, you will fail.

There are solutions, though. Depending on your skills, you may be able to create a hybrid career where you work part-time as a remote employee and part-time as a freelancer. Many people start out this way. Rather than quitting their 9–5 jobs cold turkey, they go part-time and still collect that regular paycheck until they have enough private clients to bring in steady income.

And some folks are happy to stay in that arrangement long-term. Your work does not have to match anyone else's. Just because other employees at your company work in the office doesn't mean your boss wouldn't be open to you working from home. Ask! When you're in control of your own destiny, you make the rules.

There is a third type of work-at-home career, and that's being an **entrepreneur**—building your own company that makes or sells something. Freelancers are a type of entrepreneur, but not all entrepreneurs are freelancers. Don't get hung up on the words. If you're working by your own rules, then you will benefit from this book. It doesn't matter what you call yourself, only that you're happy and productive.

You probably already have an idea about the type of role you'll most enjoy: remote employee, freelancer, or entrepreneur. All you need to do now is decide where you want to start.

You don't have to stick with it forever. You make the rules, remember?

Learn Your Craft

It should go without saying, but I'm going to say it anyway—you need to be good at what you do. Whatever you decide to do for work, be the best you can be. When you're a cog in a company machine, the company has to prove it's the best. The marketing department has to sell the clients on the company's ability to do the job. And the advertising has to convince the customers to choose them over another brand.

When you're on your own, however, you are the only cog. You *are* the machine. You are the marketing department. You will have to sell clients on your ability to do the job.

Prospective clients and employers have many options. There are plenty of freelance writers out there. Graphic designers are a dime a dozen. It seems like there's competition everywhere you look. That's the reality. So, you have to believe in your heart that you are the best person to handle that client's workload. And then you have to make the client believe you're the best person.

I'll talk about building your confidence and how to close the sale later, but for now just realize that the easiest way to nab a client or employer is to be really good at what you do. If you're just starting out and you need training, get it. Start with free videos on YouTube if you need to. Or find some online training programs or even college courses. Realize that no matter what field you're in, there's always more you can learn.

Technology evolves. Trends change. Stay on the leading edge of your industry. Know the primary players. Listen to the podcasts. Read the blogs. Make it your business to know more than the average freelancer out there. In fact, strive to know more than the top CEO out there. You will be building a reputation starting with your very first client, so make sure that it's stellar.

If you already have experience through your current or past employment, great! That all counts. Try to collect as much proof of your experience as you can. Keep your résumé up-to-date. Get testimonials from your employers. Maybe ask if you can use any good comments from your performance reviews. If you have great comments, or thank-you emails from clients you've served in the past, ask whether you can share them on your new website. Actually, that can be a great way to let them know you're starting a new venture.

Depending on the type of work you're doing, you might need special certification to sell your services legally. Do some research to find out whether the certifications are truly necessary. For example, I've had new freelance writers come to me asking if they should get certified in search engine optimization (SEO). Many courses out there offer training and certification, but the truth is you don't need a piece of paper to be an SEO writer. You simply have to learn how to do it, then go out and get clients. Writing for SEO just isn't that difficult. (Although you do need to keep current with Google's frequent algorithm changes.)

If you're already competent, or you're comfortable learning on your own, the certification may be a waste of money. But if you need to learn a skill such as SEO, and you're going to pay for training anyway, it might not be a bad idea to take that certification course to make sure you get the most up-to-date training. The more you practice your craft in the real world, the better you'll get. The better you get, the easier it will be to get clients.

Be aware that certification is a way for that training company to make money. Anyone can offer a training course and a "certificate" for completion. That doesn't necessarily mean they offer the best or most up-to-date courses. Also, price rarely correlates to the quality of the training. Just because a course is more expensive doesn't make it better. And just because a course seems like a bargain doesn't mean it's lower quality.

Research *any* training carefully, whether online or offline. Ask questions such as:

- How many people typically pass the course?
- Do you certify everyone who pays the course fee? Or do participants actually have to prove they've learned the material?
- How many graduates end up working successfully in this field?
- Will your company help me connect with potential clients?
- How often is the course upgraded with new information?
- How can I ask the instructor questions?
- Do you have testimonials from past students?

The more experience you can demonstrate, the more likely new clients are to trust you and hire you. The same goes for remote employers. So, get in the habit of keeping your skills current, and recording all your projects and clients by date. Some prospective clients will ask for a résumé or CV, and some won't. It's nice to have one on hand, though, in case they ask.

Learn your craft.

And once you've learned it, master it!

Set Up Your Workspace

Even if you plan to work while traveling or enjoying the local coffee shops, it's important to have a dedicated place at home where you can work. Personally, I get bored easily and need a variety of different places to work. Sometimes I'm typing away at the kitchen table. Sometimes I'm sprawled out on the couch with my cat purring contentedly next to me. And in the winter, I usually have my feet up in front of the woodstove with my laptop.

I can work wherever I want to, but I still have an "office" where I keep my papers, my favorite pens, and a small desk. My desk is off-limits to everyone but me. So, it keeps the kids from shuffling through my work looking for something to write on. Keeping a space dedicated to your home office also gives you certain tax benefits that may allow you to write off many common household expenses such as wireless service and other utilities.

Over the past 20 years or so, I've had all kinds of different dedicated workspaces. When the kids were young, I sometimes locked myself in my car just to get some solitude while I worked. If you're lucky enough to have a spare room, claim it! But a whole room probably isn't necessary. Most freelancers I know started with a small table in a corner somewhere—kitchens and bedrooms seem to be the most popular places. However, I don't recommend working in your bedroom, if you can help it. Working there can interfere with your sleep habits.

Whatever dedicated space you have, make it your own. You want a happy place to come to every day when it's time to work. If you have a home office, great! You can decorate to your heart's content. But even if you only have a card table, you can spruce it up with a nice tablecloth and some inspiring artwork on the wall in front of you.

If your laptop is your only office, maybe add some colorful stickers to the outside or an inspiring desktop background. It doesn't matter what you do, only that your workspace is a positive place.

It can be really difficult to separate "work time" from "family time" when you work at home. So, having a dedicated workspace can help draw the line. When you're in your office with the doors closed, you're working. When you stand up and push your chair in neatly under your desk, you're done for the day. You might not think it matters, but you'll be training your brain to switch in and out of work mode this way. This is incredibly important. When you can't switch off work mode...look out! You could be asking for health and relationship problems.

I find it's important to get out of the house frequently, or I develop a wicked case of cabin fever. Fortunately, I have to pick the kids up from school and do the grocery shopping during the week. So, I have certain tasks that force me outside. But I imagine that if I were all by myself, I could just sit inside and work for weeks on end, never talking to anyone. That's not healthy, even if you're a card-carrying introvert.

If you don't have built-in interactions with the outside world, find some! Set a weekly or monthly lunch date with a friend. Take your dog to the park. Or take a class that has nothing to do with your occupation. It can be planned or spontaneous. Just get out there and socialize now and then.

There's No Such Thing as a Perfect Office Space

As I mentioned earlier, I get bored easily. That's not good or bad, it's just how I am. When my children were young, I worked at home and dreamed of having an office somewhere. I thought it would be so cool to be able to leave the house and go work at an office, but still have control over my day.

A decade and a half later, I got that office. It wasn't anything fancy, but it was mine. A nice little space about five minutes from the kids' school. I thought it was perfect. But guess what happened? After about two months, I started finding reasons to stay home and work.

A little while later, I moved to a different office. This time, it was a gorgeous space in an old mill. It had 20-foot ceilings and the tallest windows you ever saw. There was so much light in that place. I felt very grown-up and happy. It was truly my dream space. Guess what happened? Again, I started finding reasons to stay home and work.

Now, don't get me wrong. I loved having my own space to work in. I loved that I could get out of the house. I loved that I still had control of my day. But it turns out that the look and feel of the place I work in is not nearly as important as the fact that it is *someplace else*. A few weeks in one spot and I start getting antsy. I want a change of scenery.

What I've learned about myself is that I need variety. I can work anywhere, as long as it's not for too long. After about two weeks of working at home, I need a change of pace. So, I'll head out to a coffee shop or a local park and do my work there. There are no co-working spaces near me, unfortunately. But they can be wonderful if you're lucky enough to live near one.

The lesson here is *know thyself.* Pay attention to your patterns. Your working preferences may be different. You might crave the familiar. It might be very important to your productivity to be in the same room at the same time every day. Pay attention to how you feel as you work. When do you get antsy? What do you need around you to feel productive and happy? How long can you work before you need to get up and take a break? And how can you accommodate your preferences?

You're the boss. You make the rules.

Get Your Equipment Together

It's common to delay taking the leap to work-at-home status by waiting until you can afford the best computer, the fastest internet service, and a state-of-the-art smartphone. Oh, and you'll probably need that fancy-pants software program, too.

Baloney!

Start with what you have. Borrow what you need. Upgrade when you can. When I started my freelance writing business, I couldn't afford a computer. I wanted one…badly. But it was out of the question at the time. So, I made due with a sort of hybrid typewriter that also had diskette storage capabilities. (I know… primitive, right?) I wrote magazine articles on that for about a year before we bought a real computer.

Now, realize this was before email was really viable, and journalists were sending query letters and stories on paper through the mail. These days, I wouldn't be able to get away with such a low-tech arrangement. But I could easily work on a low-end computer that connected to the internet.

Right now, I'm typing this chapter on my favorite writing tool, an AlphaSmart NEO. It's a $35 word processor that runs for about a year on three AA batteries. It's just a big keyboard with a tiny little screen. All it does is type, so there are no distractions. When I'm finished typing, I'll take it home and upload the text to my laptop.

But if I didn't have a computer, I could take it to a friend's and upload the text to Dropbox or some other cloud storage. If I needed to do research online or send email, I could always do that from the local library, if I had to. And free Wi-Fi hotspots are everywhere these days.

Do you see my point? There's almost always a creative solution to equipment issues. You simply have to start with what you have or what you can afford. As your business grows, you will be able to upgrade. Don't worry about where you're starting. Focus on where you're going.

Chances are you probably already have a home computer or laptop to use. But if not, think carefully about what your job will require in the way of storage, screen size, and other specifications. If you're a writer or customer support person, you can probably get away with a tiny laptop or tablet. But if you're a graphic designer, you may need a larger, high-resolution monitor.

Besides a computer, internet access, and a phone, you're also going to need some way to store and transfer large files online. You can't take a huge graphic-design file and send it over email. It just won't work. So, you want to use something such as Dropbox or Google Drive to store and send those files.

How will you connect to the internet? Most of your communications with clients and team members will probably happen over Zoom, GoToMeeting, or some other conferencing service. New options show up all the time—Facebook Live, UberConference—and most of them are free.

If you're going to spend money on any part of your setup, high-speed internet is worth the investment. There's nothing more embarrassing than missing a meeting with a client because your internet connection is down, or too slow to run the programs you need. If you work internationally, find the best hot spots you can, even if you have to pay for them.

What kinds of software will you use for the work you do? Can you get away with free access to Google Docs? Or do you need a monthly subscription to Adobe Creative Cloud? If you're not sure, find someone in the same field to talk to, either in person or online. Ask as many questions as you need to be sure you have the minimum equipment required to do your job.

One last thing—back up your files! There's nothing like the feeling of powering up your computer to start work and seeing the Blue Screen of Death staring you in the face. No computer lasts forever. And you never know when yours is about to bite the dust. (Or your cat is about to spill coffee all over your keyboard. Don't laugh—it happens!)

So, a reliable daily backup system is critical. Some services will back up your computer every day without you doing anything. Other types of backup require you to remember to plug in the storage device and click a button.

TAKE ACTION

Write down everything you think you'll need to do your job. Then sort the list in order of priorities. If you already have a tool that will work for now, don't spend money on a newer version until you need to. Consider creating a Wish List on Amazon or a board on Pinterest so people can purchase birthday and holiday gifts that help you build your business.

SECTION 2:

GETTING THE GIGS

Remote Employees: How to Get the Job

It's one thing to take the leap and start working from home; it's another thing to actually bring in the money. If you're an employee, you've got to land the job.

That can be easier than you might think, because it's pretty much like landing any other job. You find a company that's hiring, go through their application process, do a few interviews, and either they hire you or you start over again. Websites such as FlexJobs.com specialize in remote work and telecommuting opportunities all over the world. If you're brand new and have no idea where to look, I suggest you start there. Narrow down your list of opportunities and go for it!

The only problem with those job-directory websites is that they're public. Millions of people are looking at the same jobs, so you may have a heck of a time getting noticed. (Though the tips I share later will help.) So what's a job-seeker to do?

The best way to land a telecommuting job is to start close to home. Talk to your current boss, if you can. Is there a chance your current job could be done remotely, at least part-time? Talk to people in your network. Do they know of any remote jobs at their companies? Do they know anyone who hires people in your field? If you can get a personal introduction to a hiring manager, you're one step ahead of the masses applying for the job online. Also, your network may know of job openings before they are advertised.

In the old world, you had to compete with everyone in town who wanted that one special job. Now, you have to compete with everyone in the *world* who wants that job. So, how do you stand out and make yourself the obvious choice? Do your homework!

Research the company. What are their goals, values, and mission? You can usually find those on the company website. You might even google the company and the phrase "press release" to find out any recent initiatives they are focusing on. When you show that you're interested in the company mission, you stand out.

Research the interviewers. Once you land an interview, find out who you'll be talking to. Then look them up online and check out their LinkedIn profile. Find out what they do at the company and what might be challenging for them. If they have a personal website or blog, go check it out. Do they love dogs? Maybe you can bring that up as small talk. Did they just get married or have a baby? Congratulate them! Show an interest in the people you're talking to and you'll stand out.

Research the job. What exactly will they expect you to do? Will you need to know certain software? How did the last person perform? Maybe there are clues online. Go above and beyond what most applicants are willing to do. Offer some ideas for how you might improve the department. Is there a common problem people in that job tend to run into? Let the interviewers know you have a solution. Show you can think for yourself and take initiative.

Now, just because a position is remote doesn't necessarily mean it's a good fit for you. There are challenges with any job, remote or not, and for some companies this whole "work from home" thing is a new experiment. It's a good idea to ask a few questions of your own in the interview to uncover what kind of working environment you'll be walking into.

How do your remote teams communicate with each other and with managers? If they leave communication up to the individuals, that could mean problems down the road. You want to hear that they have clear communication channels already set up and procedures in place. Project management software isn't usually enough to keep larger teams engaged and informed. You need to know more than deadlines. You need a chat or messenger app where you can get questions answered immediately. If it takes hours or days to hear back from colleagues, imagine how long it will take to complete projects. If they have a well-oiled communication machine that's been working for years, that's a good sign.

How many employees are currently working remotely? Are they full-time or part-time? If you're the first guinea pig, that could be a serious red flag. Or it could be a really cool opportunity to set the tone for their entire program. It's important to know if you'll be expected to work with large or small teams, or if it's mostly just you and a client one-on-one. Are you comfortable working in that situation?

What are the availability expectations? You want to know if you'll be expected to handle issues 24/7/365, or whether there are certain working hours. Will you be working with international teams where time zones come into play? If you're hoping to work anywhere, anywhen, this is a critical question to ask. Sometimes people just assume that because you're working from home, you're available at all hours. You also want to find out how quickly they expect responses. If you're out playing with your kids when a rush project comes in, what's the protocol? You're designing your work environment on purpose, so make sure you get the complete picture before you accept any remote employment.

Are there any special benefits for remote employees? Often benefits like an onsite fitness center or daycare are used to attract new hires. But if you're working from home, those perks really don't matter. Find out what special perks they do have specifically for you. What's the paid-time-off policy? Will you still have to ask permission to take a vacation? Will you be expected to work year-round and never fully go off-grid?

What's the remote team culture, and how does the company keep people connected? Are there company retreats? Is there a weekly call just to catch up with each other? Are teams encouraged to post selfies with their families and share personal stories? If all the employees work in their own little bubbles and never interact with each other, that can lead to serious problems. Even if the entire company is working remotely, the team members should know each other's daily joys and struggles. They should know the names of each other's spouses and whether each person has kids. Human connection is critical to keep everyone striving toward the same goal. And connection is driven by caring. If the team members care about each other, it's much easier to work together. They can't care if they never share.

Know yourself and what kind of environment you're looking for. Then find out whether a company has a long history of using remote workers or it's something new they're trying out. Either could be a golden opportunity for you, but you need to know the situation before you walk in. You might be able to just slide into a job ready-made for you, or you might need to take some initiative and create the remote culture from scratch. As long as you know ahead of time, you're good.

TAKE ACTION

Start a research file on companies you'd like to work for. Flex-Jobs.com is a great place to find hundreds of companies that hire telecommuters. Spend some time on their websites and find their mission statements, values, and current goals. When you apply for a job, use your research file to impress the interviewers.

Freelancers: Find and Land the Gigs

If you're a freelancer or service entrepreneur, you've got to land clients. Your first…and your next…and your next. It can be a complicated process, but there are plenty of proven strategies to make it easier. I want you to hit the ground running and never look back.

So, start your client search in the easy places first, such as your current company. Could they use your services on a freelance or part-time basis? You'd be surprised how many businesses are happy to hire you back as a freelancer when they can save money on overhead and benefits and still reap the advantages of your talents.

That might sound like a rip-off. But remember, you get to skip the office politics and boring Monday meetings. You get to work on your own schedule and avoid a stressful commute. And no one is going to tell you when you can and can't take a day off.

Did you work with clients at your old company? If you haven't signed a non-compete clause, you may want to contact those clients and let them know you're no longer with your former employer. Tell them you'd be happy to help them on a contract basis, and give them your contact information. Be aware that your former employer probably won't like this. So, tread lightly, and weigh out whether it's worth any potential hassles.

How about your friends and family? Might they have a need for your services? Or do they work at a company that might be able to use you? It's possible you have no idea that your cousin

Harry's boss is in the position to offer you a huge contract, if you just ask.

Asking can be difficult, especially if your close friends and family don't support your new venture. Be courageous and do it anyway. You're not "begging" for work. You're finding out whether you can serve them in any way.

Who else do you know beyond your friends and family? How about people at church or your kid's school? Do the other moms at soccer practice know what you do? You never know, they might just need your services desperately.

Talking to people you know about your job situation doesn't have to be awkward. Start by talking about *them*. Ask them how their day was. Ask them to remind you what they do for a living. Chances are they will ask you the same questions. Then you can casually mention what you do and that you've recently started your own freelance business. They might just tell you right then that they could use you. Or they might not. Either way is fine. You're planting seeds at this point.

Over time, you might find ways to help that person, too. Let's say you're a graphic designer, and you're hanging out waiting for your daughter to finish her ballet class. You strike up a conversation with someone and find out that they need a new roof. You tell them that you happen to have a friend who's a roofer and offer to connect them. Sweet! You just served someone. You solved their problem, or at least offered one solution. The next time either your friend or that ballet mom meets someone who needs a graphic designer, who do you think they'll recommend? You!

This is how networking works. You don't push your business on people. You find out what they need and try to find a way to help them. When you do this regularly, you become known as someone generous and kind. And it's one of the best ways to get clients! In fact, depending on where you live, you might not need to do anything more than this to have all the clients you can handle.

TAKE ACTION

Make a list of all the different places you talk to people—school, church, kids' activities, the grocery store, waiting rooms—and make a commitment to strike up conversations. You don't have to talk in detail about what you do, just get in the habit of talking to people. You never know where a conversation will lead.

Attract New Clients on Autopilot

Early on, you might have some ups and downs in terms of your income. Sometimes freelancers struggle for years going from having many clients to no clients, or having a steady income to having little or no income. It's frustrating and scary, especially if you have a family to support.

If you want to avoid that outrageous income-roller-coaster ride, you must learn some marketing skills. If you're unfamiliar with marketing, it can seem intimidating at first. But it doesn't have to be. Marketing is nothing more than letting people know what you do and that you're available to help them. You're just getting the word out there. No big deal.

There are all kinds of different ways to do this. For this reason, it's really easy to fall into the marketing trap, where you're constantly studying the newest marketing strategies. You're "really busy" researching and implementing, but you never really get out there into the world.

For example, some freelancers will tinker with their websites for years, refusing to advertise to clients until their website is "perfect." Well, news flash—your website will never be perfect! You will always be tweaking the copy and adding testimonials and changing the pictures.

Working on your website isn't going to pay the bills. Clients pay the bills. Your website can help you get clients, but not if it's never finished. The same goes for social media. Yes, having a presence on Facebook or Instagram can help you get clients.

But if you're spending hours every day trying to craft the perfect posts, you're not actually getting anywhere.

If your business depends on a constant flow of new clients, you need to build marketing systems that will bring you those people while you're busy working on actual paying projects. This idea is called marketing automation, and it can completely revolutionize your business.

Again, don't be tempted to spend your whole life studying and implementing different types of automation. (It's really easy to spend *way* too much money on automation software.) Be smarter than that. Just stick to the basics at first.

You don't need much really. You need…

1. A way for people to find you
2. A way to build trust with those people
3. A way for them to contact you

You can achieve all three goals with a simple website, email, and some social media.

Your Website: A website is not optional. You must have one! The first thing a potential client typically does is look you up online. You need a professional representation of your business. At a bare minimum, you should have a home page, an about page, and a contact page. If you like, you can put each of these components on a single page. Just be sure your site addresses the following questions as quickly as possible:

- Who are you?
- Who do you help?
- What do you help with?
- How can people get in touch with you?

Your home page should clearly state who you help and what you can do for them. This is easily accomplished with a simple headline formula.

- I help _____ with _____ so that _____.
- I _____ for _____ so they can _____.
- Do you have trouble _____? I can help!

Here are some examples:

- I help restaurant owners with social media so they can fill more tables on slow nights.
- I write blog posts for entrepreneurs, so they can focus on serving their customers.
- Do you have trouble managing your appointments? I can help!

Once you've clearly explained who you help and how you help them, all that's left is to tell the website visitor a little bit about yourself and let them know how they can get in touch with you, by email or phone, for example.

Next, you need to build some trust. You need to prove to your prospective client that you can handle their project. Testimonials are a great way to do this. You can add these written or video endorsements anywhere on your website, but it's a good idea to have at least one on your home page. Providing samples of your work is another great way to build trust by showing what you can do. As you gain more experience, be sure to showcase your best and most recent samples. Your about page is another trust builder. Tell your story. Help the visitor connect with you on a more personal level.

You can also build trust through a blog. Now, before you say, "But Julie! I don't have time to write a blog!" I get it. Blogging is one of those tasks I put below cleaning my bathroom or shoveling snow. But there are a few tricks you should know. Just because it's a blog doesn't mean you have to call it that. The word "blog" carries with it an expectation that you will update it regularly—monthly, weekly, or perhaps even daily. Followers will check to see how recently you posted. If it has been a while, they may think you're not reliable. So unfair!

Here's the trick: either remove the dates from your posts or name your blog "Articles" instead. An article is a stand-alone piece. It doesn't carry the same expectation of continual updates that blog posts do. So, instead of the word "blog" on your navigation bar, just substitute the word "articles." Now, all you have to do is write up a couple of helpful posts and you're done.

The other thing about blogs is that they don't have to be text-based. You can create a video or a podcast and add it to your blog instead of a regular post. Even though I write for a living, I really dislike blogging. (Don't ask me why—it's just a thing with me.) But I love to make podcasts and embed them on my blog. No text required.

What should you discuss? Find 10 problems your potential clients have and create a post for each one. Just solve the problem for them, don't try to sell your services. Or come up with 10 frequently asked questions and answer them in a series of posts. You're serving the visitor by teaching them something helpful. By doing that, you're building a great foundation of trust and expertise.

The next thing you need is a way for people to contact you. I like to include both an email address and a phone number on every page. I don't want people searching around the site for a way to get in touch with me. Make it easy. If you're nervous about putting your actual phone number online, you can create a free Google Voice number at voice.google.com. Then have the messages forwarded wherever you want.

Automated Email Sequence: This is where your marketing gets really slick! It's also where you may be tempted to spend a lot of money. If you're just starting out, bootstrap it. Companies such as MailChimp and AWeber are inexpensive and will handle your marketing just fine. When your business grows and requires more sophistication, you can graduate to platforms such as Infusionsoft, ONTRAPORT, or my favorite, ClickFunnels.

The idea is to lead your website visitors through a series of steps that helps them and also gives you the opportunity to send them marketing emails. Here's the process you'll lead them through.

1. The site visitor sees a free offer like a report or checklist on your website that helps them solve some small problem.

2. They give you their email address in return for that information. By doing that, they are subscribing to your email list.

3. You deliver the free report and thank them for subscribing to your list.

4. Over the next few days, *automated* emails are sent out, helping them come to the conclusion that they should hire you.

5. From time to time, you send out email newsletters. They will receive these until they unsubscribe from your list.

Please note that it is illegal to send unsolicited email, and you're not allowed to send bulk-marketing emails from your regular email server. That's why automation companies exist, to keep you in line with spam laws.

There is a bit of tech involved in setting up this email marketing automation. But all email providers have wonderful video tutorials that will walk you through how to set everything up. You might need to spend a little time to get everything working properly. But once it's done, you can just forget about it. Your marketing system will be all set up to bring you prospective clients while you're busy working on your paying projects.

Social Media: People often ask me, "Which social media channels should I use? There are so many!" I tell them they should have a basic profile set up on all the major platforms, including Facebook, Twitter, Instagram, LinkedIn, and Pinterest. Having a profile just means you set up the page with your picture, a description of your business, a link to your website, and a few pieces of content. You don't have to actively engage on every network. Just tell people where they can interact with you. If you love Instagram, tell people that on Facebook and Twitter. Just write, "Hey! Thanks for finding me. I'm more active on Instagram. Come find me there."

Engage with people on the platform you think they are most likely to be on. Personally, I love Twitter. I get the best engagement there. When choosing your favorite, keep your target audience in mind—especially their ages. Facebook tends to attract people over the age of 35. Instagram tends to skew toward the younger crowd. The newer the platform, the more likely the younger crowds will flock there in search of the "next big thing." Add social media icons to your website and link them to your profiles so people will know where to follow you.

And try to use the same profile picture across all your accounts. You want your face to become familiar to your prospects.

Now you have a way for people to find you (your social media and website). You have built trust with testimonials and quality blog posts (articles). And you have a way for people to contact you (email and phone). Congratulations! You've got a basic marketing system in place. From now on, all your marketing efforts such as speaking engagements, guest blogging, and networking meetings have a "home base" where you can send people. Anytime you're talking or writing about your business, include a link to your website.

You Need One More Thing

A website, no matter how well designed, isn't going to bring you clients all by itself. No one will know your site is there if you don't promote it. The marketing term is "driving traffic," which just means you need a way to send people to your site on a regular basis. There are hundreds of ways to do this; some cost money and some don't. I recommend you start by promoting your blog posts on your favorite social media channels. By linking back to the original post, you'll be sending traffic to your website.

Another free traffic strategy is to write guest blog posts on other websites that already have lots of visitors. Include a link to your website in your author bio at the end of the post. If people are interested in learning more, they'll click the link and land on your site.

Some other traffic generators include:

- Being interviewed on a popular podcast or radio show
- Writing articles for your local newspaper or industry trade magazines

- Handing out business cards
- Mentioning your website whenever you speak to groups
- Teaching workshops or classes (online or offline)
- Posting helpful videos on YouTube

If you need more ideas, simply google "website traffic strategies" and you'll have enough information to last you the rest of your life. Pick one or two ideas to start with, and do them consistently. That's more important than trying every single strategy out there.

Ongoing Marketing Activities

Once your home base and automation are set up, you have a great system for collecting leads from your website. But there are other forms of marketing you'll want to use, too. I tell my students, "You can't fail at marketing, you can only fail to DO your marketing." Pick something that works, and DO IT. Consistently. Every day, if you can. This is how you keep the flow of steady clients coming in, and how you avoid the feast-or-famine roller-coaster ride.

There are so many different activities you can try, and you don't have to do them all. I'm going to list a few of my favorites here. Feel free to research other ideas on your own. The goal is to pick a few activities you enjoy and do them consistently. Every now and then, just for fun, try an activity you're NOT comfortable with. Step outside your comfort zone and see what happens. You might just strike gold.

In-Person Networking: Start with who you know. Whenever you're out and about, strike up conversations with people. This might be a bit uncomfortable at first, but it does get easier with practice. And it's so important to talk to people regularly. They can't hire you if they don't know what you do.

Start by talking about *them.* Compliment them on their shoes, or notice something they're carrying. Are you at a soccer game with your kids? Talk to the other parents about what a great game the kids are having. You don't have to start out with an agenda—just be nice to people.

Then you can casually turn the conversation to what they do for a living. If you already know, you can just ask, "How's the job going these days?" Most likely, they'll respond by asking how your job is going. That's your chance to mention that you're working from home now helping people with XYZ. Mention that you're accepting new clients right now, if they know anyone who could use help.

Then drop the subject, unless they ask questions and want to continue talking about it. You just want to plant a seed. Don't try to sell them anything, unless they want you to. If they ask more questions, answer them. But other than that, just be cool.

There are some networking situations where people will expect you to tell them what you do and whether you're accepting new clients. Events hosted by your local chamber of commerce, special group meetups, or business roundtables are great places to do some in-person networking.

Make it a point to give more advice and assistance than you ask for, and people will really enjoy talking with you. Open your ears and really listen. Are they struggling with something? Can you offer some solid advice or helpful resources, or connect them with someone you trust? They'll appreciate that you're helping them out, and they'll often go out of their way to help you in return.

If you live in a city, or even a decent-sized town, in-person networking might be all the marketing you ever have to do. However, if you're like me and you live in the middle of nowhere, you're going to have to travel a bit to network face-to-face. It's worth taking the time to go meet people, even if all you're doing at first is getting used to talking about what you do.

Conferences and Seminars: When I was starting out, I found most of my copywriting clients by attending conferences and seminars. By the time I paid for airfare, hotels, and food, it was a pretty big expense. But I always came home with more than enough work to make up for it.

I've learned a few tricks for being successful at conference marketing. The most important thing is to go to the conferences where your *clients* will be, not your peers. If you're a writer, you're probably not going to get a lot of business at a writers conference. You need to go where the attendees are likely to need writers, such as a business conference (if you're a business writer), or a medical symposium (if you're a medical writer). If you're an editor, though, a writers conference might work out well for you.

If you don't want to (or can't) attend the conference itself (for example, because you're not a doctor), you can still recruit clients. Book a room in the hotel and set yourself up in the bar. Look for people just coming out of the meetings, or pay attention to those little name badges. Then just strike up a conversation with someone who looks receptive. It's best if you can attend the conference, but that's not always possible. So, meeting the people outside the event can work as a last resort.

Asking for Referrals: The best client is a current client, and the second best is a referral. These days, the few clients I do take on are almost always referrals from someone I've worked with before. Whenever you find yourself in need of clients, make it a practice to ask your current or past ones if they might know someone who could use your services. Very often, they will. It's tempting to think that clients will offer referrals on their own, but the truth is they don't always think to do so.

Guest Blogging: Another way to market yourself is to post on someone else's blog. Content marketing is huge right now.

Every company needs to come up with regular fresh, engaging content. If you offer to write a blog post or create a video for someone else, they will often happily accept. That's one more post they don't have to write!

You can use this technique with companies you hope to work for and/or blogs where your target clients are likely to read your post. If you're a graphic designer, for example, you might offer to create a post for a digital agency near you. By showcasing your abilities and strengths, it's possible they might recruit you or send you their overflow work. You might also offer to create a post for a popular business-news website where other local businesses will see you and possibly hire you.

How will they know how to reach you? Guest posts typically have an author bio at the bottom of the post where you can tell people what you do and how they can contact you. Link to your website from here, and include your business phone number, if it's appropriate. If there's room, sneak in a short testimonial, too.

Podcast Interviews: Appearing on a popular podcast or radio show can bring you work as well. Just be sure the audience includes people who might be in a position to hire you. When the host asks you what you do or where people can find you, be sure to mention exactly what you do, who you help, and your website link. Make it easy for listeners to find you.

And don't underestimate the power of small podcasts. One of the first times I was a guest on a small podcast, I didn't expect anything to come from it. I figured it was just practice for when I was on bigger shows. Two days after it aired, I had a $75,000 ghostwriting contract! Then, about a year and a half later, the host of the show actually hired me to coach him through writing his book. So, you never know. Keep putting yourself out there.

Social Media Engagement: Almost every freelancer or work-at-home entrepreneur I know thinks they spend too much time on social media. It's often the goof-off technique of choice. But social media can also be a great way to meet and engage with potential clients, if you're strategic.

My favorite platform is Twitter. When I was doing a lot of copywriting, some of my best clients found me there. I spent some time chatting with them, and then they would often connect with me on LinkedIn, where they would message me about work opportunities. I didn't just get one-off jobs this way, either. One client found me from a single tweet. He called me, we hit it off, and he hired me for a $25,000 project.

Your platform of choice might be Instagram or Facebook. Go where your potential clients are hanging out most often. And remember, social media is about being social. It's about talking with people and helping them, not selling your services overtly.

Press Releases and Media Mentions: There's an old saying that advertising is what you pay for, and publicity is what you *pray* for. That's still true today, whether you're talking about online media such as blogs and podcasts or offline media such as radio, TV, and newspapers. Learn to write press releases and media pitches. Then let the media know when you've got something newsworthy to report.

What's newsworthy?

- Opening a new business
- Getting a high-profile client
- Offering solutions for a local problem
- Sponsoring charity events and other community involvement

If you google the phrase "press release," you'll see all sorts of examples. The goal is to get journalists to pay attention to you and write about you. They won't pick up every release you send. It might take a year or more before you send them something that's interesting to their audiences. That's okay. Send the releases anyway.

TAKE ACTION

Write down five ways you can market your business on an ongoing basis. Then schedule a time in your calendar to do at least one activity per week. If you schedule it, you're more likely to actually do it.

Collect Killer Testimonials

Potential clients don't like to take risks with their projects. They want to know that you can do the work, do it right the first time, and that there won't be any drama or difficulties on your end. And guess what? They don't want to hear all that from you. Well, they do. But they also need to hear it from at least one third party. This is called social proof. If they see that someone else hired you and had a great experience, they are more likely to hire you.

So, you need testimonials. A testimonial is just an endorsement—someone saying something nice about you and/or your work. It's best if that somebody is an actual client. Which leads to a bit of a problem. How do you get testimonials if you don't have any clients yet?

A client is a client. How much they paid for your services is not important. So, when you're just starting out, you can work for a lower rate or even for free in return for a testimonial. Maybe your local school system or animal shelter could use your services. Nonprofits are a great choice because you'll feel good helping them, and you'll end up with a nice testimonial from a legitimate business. All you need is one or two solid testimonials at the beginning. So, please don't get stuck working cheap or free for too long.

Now, there are good testimonials and there are *amazing* testimonials, which can sell you better than practically any other marketing strategy. You want the amazing ones! How do you get them? Well, there's a little bit of strategy behind it. Take a look at the testimonial below.

"Sarah's work was top-notch. She finished quickly and delivered exactly what I needed."

Pretty good, right? But what if it read like this?

A Real Lifesaver!

> "I was in a jam and didn't know where to turn. My assistant had a family emergency and had to leave town in the middle of a major project. I knew I couldn't handle the project myself, and I didn't have time to search around for a suitable replacement. So, I hopped online, found Sarah, and hoped for the best.
>
> Oh my, what a lifesaver! Sarah's work was top-notch. She finished quickly and delivered exactly what I needed. If you need an assistant, stop looking! Hire Sarah. You won't regret it."

That one sounds a lot better, doesn't it? Don't you just want to call Sarah and hire her right now? (I do!) Imagine having a testimonial like that on your website.

Here's the thing: people are busy. And most of them don't like to write. So, if you ask a client for a testimonial, they'll probably say, "Sure, absolutely. I'll write something up and send it over." If you're lucky, they'll follow through. But most of the time, even the most well-meaning people will have a hard time complying. Either they will write something up quickly, such as the first example above. Or they'll put it off because they don't know what to say.

So make it easy for them. Tell them that if they will take two minutes to answer a few quick questions, you will write up the testimonial and then get their approval to use it. They can either type out the answers in an email, or make a voice recording if that's easier.

Hmm, just answer a couple of questions? That's easy, right? I've never had anyone say no to this. Ask them some variation on the following questions:

- Why were you seeking help with _____ in the first place?
- How did you find me?
- What were you expecting when you hired me?
- What was your experience working with me?
- What results did you experience?
- Would you recommend me to others? Who else could use my services?
- Is there anything else you'd like to add?

By asking these specific questions, you get a more complete picture of the experience. Most people are hesitant or nervous when they hire someone new. That's true for your client answering the questions, and it's true for any prospective clients reading the testimonial. So, being up front about that in the testimonial will go a long way toward selling your prospect.

They will read the words, "I was nervous about hiring someone on the internet," and they'll think, *Yeah, I'm a little nervous about that, too.* Then they'll read the rest of the testimonial and see that it worked out great with you, and their fears will be eased.

Once your client has answered your questions, you have everything you need to write an amazing testimonial for yourself. Take their answers and write out a story about their experience. Be sure to include *how they felt* before, during, and after the work was done. Take the most powerful part of the testimonial and make it a bold headline (as I did in the example above). Then all that's left is to send the final testimonial back to the client for approval. They will almost always approve it because you're using their words, even if you had to tweak them a little to make the sentences fit together.

Try to get this done within a day or two, if possible. The more time that goes by between the end of the project and the final approval, the harder it is to get a testimonial. Don't let it linger. If the client is always traveling or in meetings, have him schedule five minutes with you on the phone. Ask him the questions and record his answers. That can often yield the best stories, and makes it much easier for them. You can either use recording software on your phone, or use a free service such as UberConference or Voxer.

Any testimonial is better than none, but try to get that before–during–after story if you can. The more details you can include, the better. Ask the client how he felt. Emotions sell! How did he feel before working with you? How did he feel while working with you? How does he feel now, after working with you? If you can get audio or video testimonials from your clients, even better. There's just something about the human voice that's so much more believable than text on a screen.

Once you've got the testimonial, what do you do with it? Post it anywhere and everywhere it makes sense to do so! Some people put testimonials on their websites and that's it. What a waste. Put them wherever people might find you.

- Business cards
- Byline or author bio
- Directory listings
- Email signature
- Flyers
- Online forum signatures
- Social media profiles

There might not be room on your business card or Twitter profile for a whole three-paragraph testimonial. That's okay. Pull out the most persuasive sentence or two and just use that. The point is, you want social proof anywhere a potential client might find you. Someone else's words about you are worth 100 times what you say about yourself.

TAKE ACTION

Do you have any past clients who could give you a good testimonial? Write down anyone you can think of, then contact them and ask. You might even end up with a new project!

Anchor Your Clients:
Under-Promise and Over-Deliver

Once you've worked hard to get a client interested, you want them to stick with you, right? It's so much easier to continue serving clients who already know and trust you than to continually search for new ones. So, you want to anchor your clients. You want them to be so happy with you that they would never even think of going someplace else to get what they need.

It can be really tempting to charge too little and promise too much just to get the first gig. Almost everyone new to this game does it. I did it. All my freelance friends have done it. We try to lure a client in with a great bargain. We think they will appreciate that we're so cheap. Well, guess what? It can backfire on you—for several reasons.

Believe it or not, quoting a rate that's too low will scare away the really good clients. They will think you don't know what you're doing, or you can't handle their very important project. All because you're too cheap. The best clients want someone they can trust to do the job right—on time, without a lot of drama. And they know that high quality costs more.

So, even when you're just starting out, don't try to be the cheapest option. You can always negotiate down if you want to. But by charging appropriate rates, you'll be positioning yourself as a highly paid professional, rather than a newbie who's desperate to get a gig.

It's also tempting to over-promise and build up the scope of the project until you have so much to do that you hate this new freelance thing. You'll be bogged down with so much work, there won't be time for those nice walks in the park you were dreaming about when you had that J-O-B.

Even worse, you might think you can't handle this life. You might tell yourself you're not good enough. Those little voices in your head will say, *See? We told you this wouldn't work.* When the truth is, you simply over-promised what you could deliver to the client in the time allotted.

Take a good look at what they need you to do. Assess how long you think it will take, and tack on at least 10% more time. Then charge accordingly. Being realistic about your time, skills, and amount of money you need to collect will serve you well in the long run.

Will you lose some clients? Maybe. But in my experience, the bargain-seeker clients tend to be the biggest pains in the butt anyway. They come up with the most drama—such as paying late or not at all. They have the most unreasonable demands, such as unlimited revisions. You deserve the great clients. The ones who respect you and your skills. The ones who will pay you on time and hire you again and again. Those people are willing to pay a little more and wait a little longer to get the work done right.

If you do happen to finish a project early, or come under budget—bonus! That's called over-delivering, and clients *love* it. If you really want to impress them, you can give a little extra.

Did they hire you to write a blog post? You could throw in some social media posts to promote it. Did they hire you to design a logo? Maybe you could throw that logo on a business card template as a little extra. The Cajun culture calls this *lagniappe*. It means "a little extra." Give that extra attention, and your clients will love you! They'll come back for more and happily send you referrals, too.

TAKE ACTION

What "little extra" can you offer your clients? Write down a few ideas and implement them on your next project. Don't tell the client ahead of time. Make it a happy surprise, and it will be even more meaningful.

Model Successful People

Whatever you want to do, someone else has probably done it before you, and done it successfully. When you're first starting out (or if you're stuck and want to move up to the next level), look around for those success stories. You can find these people being interviewed on podcasts and guest blogging for larger websites.

Find out what their businesses look like. How are they marketing their services? Are they charging by the hour or by the project? How much are they charging? Do they list their past clients on their websites? What do their profiles on the freelance job directories look like? All this is valuable information for your own business.

Your goal here is not to copy them. It's to *model* what's working. *Do not* go to a competitor's website and rip off their work! Don't copy their home page. And don't use their package descriptions verbatim. But do notice what their home page looks like. Are they using video or text? Do they have prices on the website or not? Do they make prospective clients fill out an application? How are they advertising their services elsewhere online? Are they active offline in their community? Perhaps they attend certain seminars or conferences.

If they are successful, then they've figured some things out. You can learn from them. Just don't copy or infringe on their intellectual property. If you're lucky, you might be able to chat with them about how they got started. You could score some great advice. I have fledgling freelancers contact me from all over the world asking for advice on various topics (which is partly why I'm writing this book in the first place). As long as they are respectful and don't make unreasonable demands on my time, I'm usually happy to answer their questions.

There really is no competition in the world. There are more than enough gigs for everyone! There are always more clients. You will have times when you won't believe that's true, but just accept it. If you believe there are plenty of clients out there and plenty of employers hiring remote workers, then your only job is to go out and find them.

One note of caution—don't compare yourself to someone who has much more experience. Even though that other person might seem light-years ahead, you have no idea what they've gone through, what challenges they've faced, or how long they've been working to get where they are. "Compare and despair" is a very real problem when you're starting out. It's easy to look at a successful competitor and think…

> *I'll never make that much money.*
>
> *I'll never have that much talent.*
>
> *I can't believe how much they can charge!*
>
> *Where in the world do they find clients who will pay that much?*

Focus on yourself. Wherever you are at this moment is perfect. As long as you're moving forward, even at a snail's pace, you are going to be just fine. Don't envy your competitors; befriend them.

TAKE ACTION

Who are the successful people working in your industry? The bloggers, the podcast hosts, the YouTube stars, the people speaking at conferences? Write down a few names and go research them. Really dig into their careers. How did they get where they are? What marketing and advertising methods do they use? How long have they been in business? What does their website look like? What kinds of content do they produce? How often do they produce it?

Then think of some ways you can do something similar in your business.

Stand Out in a Competitive Market

No matter what kind of work you do, whether you are freelance or employed, there are thousands of other qualified candidates for the jobs you want. Remote working means that anyone, anywhere can apply for the same job. How do you compete?

You have to stand out somehow. Be unique. Find something that makes you memorable among all the pages and pages of profiles and résumés. Here are a few ideas.

Get a referral from your network. You're always going to be a step ahead if you can get a personal introduction or referral from someone inside the hiring organization. LinkedIn is a great tool for finding relationships you didn't know existed. Just do a search for the person or company you're going to be speaking with, and LinkedIn will tell you who in your network is connected. Who knows? Your Aunt Sally might be best friends with the hiring manager. Sweet!

Be specific. Use numbers and metrics when you can. How many projects did you complete for your last company? What were the engagement metrics? What percentage of people opened the email you wrote? You can include this information with your résumé and mention it during interviews.

Another way to be specific is to think back on your experience that might be relevant. If you're talking with a potential client about a web development job for a hospital, and you've designed six other hospital websites in the past—bring it up! If the client is concerned about your ability to learn a certain software, mention that you had to learn new software on your last job, too. And you had no trouble quickly getting up to speed. (Assuming that's true, of course.)

Use video. Faces and voices will always stand out against words on a résumé. Videos can be a great way to stand out and make an impression. They don't have to be professionally produced. Just a simple recording on your phone will do. You can make video résumés, video welcome messages for your website, and even embed videos in email communication. (You do that by adding a screenshot of the video with a Play arrow over it in the email, and link it to the video on YouTube or your website.)

Ask questions. People are naturally self-centered. We all think about ourselves first. It's just human nature. Use that to your advantage by making your conversation mostly about *them*. Most people going into an interview wait to be asked questions and talk about why they would be the best candidate for the job. Instead, turn the interview around so *you* ask the questions.

"What are your goals? What are you hoping the project will accomplish? What's your timeline? How will the work I do help fulfill your mission?"

The more you know about them, the easier it will be to tailor your proposal to exactly what they need.

Match your samples to the client. When I was writing articles for different niches such as healthcare and fitness, I had the phrase "Samples available on request" on my website. When a potential client asked for samples, I sent them the most relevant ones first. If a client is in the financial industry, and all your samples are fitness-oriented, they could skip over you.

Do some research ahead of time. Know something about the company or person you're talking to. A five-minute review of their website can tell you a lot. If you're the only candidate who took the time to learn the company mission and values, you will definitely stand out. For example, if the client loves dogs and has them plastered all over her website, ask about them. Doing a little research allows you to make a personal connection. And personal connections are remembered.

Answer the phone. Have you ever tried to call someone and been sent directly to voice mail? Frustrating, isn't it? It makes you wonder, *Is it me? Are they screening calls and they just don't want to talk to me?* Don't be that guy! Be better than that. If a prospect is calling you, they need you…probably right away. So, don't make them wait. Answer the phone right away, with a cheery voice. One of the publishers I work with answers the phone every time with, "This is David. I can help!" I love that so much. It makes me smile before I even say a word. If you can't answer immediately for some reason (like when you're driving), call them back as soon as you possibly can. The same goes for email and even social media messages.

People used to advise freelancers *not* to answer their phones. It was deemed "good positioning" to appear too busy to pick up the phone. You must be really in demand if you can't answer the phone. That might have been the case years ago, but today it's what everybody does. If you're trying to stand out, do what everybody else *won't*. I've advertised projects on freelance websites and hired the first person who got back to me. Not because they were particularly better than anyone else, but because they were ready to go when I was.

We are living in a global marketplace. So, think about how time zone differences might affect your business. If your clients tend to come from a drastically different time zone, or you travel a lot, you might want to set up an email autoresponder. When someone contacts you, have an automatic email reply letting them know where you are and when they can expect a response. That way, they won't be left wondering whether you even received their message.

Even if you're a remote employee and aren't looking for clients, answer the phone. Call back promptly. Return emails as soon as you can. Good communication helps you stand out as someone who's reliable. And that's a good thing!

Follow up. The freelance and remote-working fields move pretty quickly. Follow-up is so important. After an interview, send a handwritten thank-you note, and maybe even a little gift such as a Starbucks gift card. Even if you're not offered that gig, at least you will be remembered. Check back in six months or so, and you might be hired for the next project. Work hard to make a good impression and connect with people, and keep those connections active whether or not they land you immediate work.

Compete on Online Job Directories

There are plenty of websites where you can find freelance and remote-working gigs. Some people will tell you they're an easy way to find work. Others will tell you those sites are worthless because they're full of people who undercut you and expect you to work for peanuts. They are both right…and both wrong.

When I was starting out as a freelance writer, there was no internet. Email wasn't even a thing yet. I wrote query letters to magazine editors and mailed them. I worked for local businesses in town, writing articles for the newspaper and selling advertising. So, when I discovered there were these things called websites, and some of them actually posted jobs I could do, I was thrilled!

Getting paid $35 to write an article for a website was better than the $25 I earned to sit through a two-hour school board meeting and summarize it for the newspaper. I was happy just writing away with anything they sent me. But that was almost 20 years ago, and things have changed.

These days, we have to compete in a global marketplace. And someone in Bangladesh can afford to write an article for a lot less than I can. But that doesn't mean I can't compete on sites such as Upwork or Freelancer. The fact is, many employers are not simply looking for the cheapest option. It's more important that you speak fluent English (or French or German or whatever…). It's more important that you can take direction and do the project right the first time. It's more important that you are trustworthy and honest. There are plenty of reasons a client might choose you over another freelancer. So, don't feel as if you have to be the lowest-priced option.

Freelance job sites and databases are great places to start looking for work, especially when you need samples and testimonials to show other prospective clients. But don't limit yourself to just those sites. You've already learned about other ways to get clients. Try them all, and see what works best for you.

Are you looking for permanent or part-time remote work? As I mentioned earlier, FlexJobs.com has a huge variety of remote and telecommuting jobs, not just the usual suspects. Here are a few other sites you might want to check out.

- 99designs.com (graphic design)
- Freelancer.com
- Guru.com
- Outsource.com
- PeoplePerHour.com
- SimplyHired.com (remote and on-location jobs)
- Toptal.com (as in "top talent"; for software engineers and developers)
- Upwork.com
- VirtualVocations.com

Tips for Winning on Competitive Sites

The biggest drawback to online job directories is that they are so competitive. There are sometimes thousands of qualified candidates for every gig posted. So, how do you stand out? How do you get hired?

If you've researched this problem, you've probably come across lots of blog posts complaining about how hard it is to find decent work this way. Yet there are plenty of freelancers who make six-figure incomes from the exact same sites. Are they just lucky? Probably not. They've just taken time to learn the system. They've figured out how to be successful. If you don't land the first few gigs, so what? Keep trying.

Here are a few tips to put you ahead of most of the competition you'll face.

Get found. Your future clients are looking for you on these sites. Your first objective is to be found. That means your profile needs to show up when they search. They can't hire you if they don't know you're there.

Think about who might be searching for you on that site. What keywords will they type in to find you? Include as many of these keywords in your profile as possible. Include different kinds of projects you can do, and include the software programs you're comfortable using. If I'm searching for a graphic designer, I might type in "logo" or I might just type in "photoshop." The more keywords you include in your profile, the more likely you'll display on more job searches.

You'll also be found more often if you have a good track record. The freelancers with the right keywords and the highest ratings tend to show up first. So, try to get some ratings right away. One way to do that is to work a project for someone you know through that site. Let's say your cousin needs a website. Have her post the project on the directory site, hire you through the site, then give you a five-star rating and a great testimonial (assuming you earned them).

Build trust. Once a potential client finds you and clicks on your profile, your next (and most important) mission is to build trust as quickly as possible. That starts with your profile picture. Make sure you have a friendly, smiling picture of yourself. People want to work with other *people*, not cartoon avatars or pictures of your cat. Then be sure to fill out your profile completely. Answer every single question as best you can. Include a résumé and your best samples. If you've worked for high-profile clients (household names such as Nike, Coke, or IBM), include their logos in your description. Finally, add testimonials to your profile. Other people's experiences can go a long way toward convincing a new client to hire you.

Encourage contact. Just because someone glances at your profile and likes it doesn't mean they'll initiate contact with you. It's a good idea to encourage them by writing "Get in touch" or "Let's talk about your project" somewhere in the profile. You can even give precise instructions such as, "Scroll up, click the Contact button, and tell me more about your needs and goals."

Ask questions. Once they contact you, it's time to find out what's really important to them. Why are they contracting out for this project? When do they need it? Speed is often a big deal to people hiring on these sites. If they had time to wait, they could have just gone to an agency or possibly waited for it to be done in-house.

The more questions you ask, the clearer picture you'll get about how you can help them. Here's a sales tip: Use their own words in your response. If they say, "I need this logo because we've changed direction in the company." You might say back, "It can be really hard when a company changes direction. I can design a great new logo that will match your new direction perfectly."

It might sound contrived to you, but it tells the client you're listening. I've found if I try to paraphrase the information they give me, they will sometimes think I don't understand. But if I use their exact words and phrases, they feel we have a connection and that I "get" them. That connection goes a long way toward making the sale.

Seal the deal. When you're bidding on a gig or replying to a request, focus on the value to the customer. They might value time saved, quality work, or a drama-free experience. Let them know you offer those things. Don't assume they're shopping for the lowest price. Most of the time, other considerations are more important.

If it's a long-term gig, you might offer to do a paid test project. A low-risk audition might be just the thing to get you in the door. Finally, ask for the job. Say something like, "I'd love to help you. Shall we work together on this?"

Get feedback. Once the work is finished, leverage your efforts for the future. Make sure every client gives you a five-star review and writes some positive comments about your work. They usually won't bother if you don't ask them to. When you deliver the work, tell them you enjoyed working with them and that you'd love it if they'd take the time to leave a positive review and comments. When they do, you might go one step further and ask if it's okay to share their comments on your website.

At this point, you can also ask for more work.

"Thanks for the opportunity, Mrs. Jones. Is there anything else I can help you with right now?"

If she says yes, sweet! You just got another gig. If she says no, thank her and let her know she can always contact you directly through the site for future work.

Over time, you'll develop favorite ways for attracting new clients. But in the beginning, try them all! The larger directories such as Upwork and Freelancer are more competitive, but they also have more potential clients posting jobs. New directories pop up every week, and that's great. If you get in early, there will be less competition. However, no one knows about them yet. So, you may not find much action there. You never know, though, so sign up for lots of job directories and see what happens.

TAKE ACTION

Create a master profile for the various online directories. Remember to use keywords and search phrases to increase your chance of being found. Use this master document to save time whenever you set up a new account on a job site.

Demonstrate Your Expertise

If you've been working a corporate job for years, or you have an advanced degree in a particular subject area, then you're an expert at what you do. Even if you've only been out on your own for a little while, all those years of experience still count. One way to start attracting those higher-paying gigs is to demonstrate your expertise somehow. Prove to people that you are a leader in your field. How?

- Write a book.
- Start a podcast.
- Keep a blog.
- Write guest articles for your industry association's newsletter or trade magazine.

If you are the one giving advice through a blog or some other media, you will be perceived as an authority on your subject.

Answer those frequently asked questions. Solve the common problems you see clients struggling with. It's all content. And it doesn't matter if you prefer to write, shoot a video, or record your voice. Pick whichever method suits you best and run with it.

You might be thinking, *But I don't have time to start a podcast or write a book!* Maybe not. It does take a while to gain traction and get noticed with some of these avenues. So, how can you still use media to demonstrate your expertise?

How about appearing on someone else's podcast? (Sometimes all you have to do is ask.) What if you wrote one or two articles for a company you'd really like to work for? Could you interview other experts in your field? Simply by sharing the spotlight with a known expert, you gain additional credibility. It's called the Halo Effect. You gain credibility just by interviewing someone who is a known expert. And that credibility can go a long way toward convincing a client to hire you. It's all about trust with clients. They have to trust you. And the more credibility factors you have in your favor, the better.

Whatever you do, be sure to add a bio including what you do, who you help, and a link to your website. That's how people find you.

Price Your Work Appropriately

You'll need to decide early on whether you're going to charge by the hour or by the project (or some other method). If you're a remote employee, chances are you'll just go by what the job description says. Most employers are used to paying by the hour, so that's probably what you'll be offered. And that's great.

However, if you're working for a variety of clients, think hard about which model you want to use. They both have pros and cons. Let's say you charge $50 an hour. That sounds like a great deal until you realize that you work quickly. If it takes you 30 minutes to complete a project, you'll only take home $25 for it. But if you charge $50 for the whole project, you would be able to finish two projects in that same hour—effectively making $100 an hour. Charging by the hour makes you dependent on the clock. You can only earn as much as you work. When you charge by the project, it doesn't matter how long it takes to complete. The faster you work, the more you can earn.

On the other hand, if you have a very large project worth tens of thousands of dollars, it can sound better to the client if you're quoting $50 an hour, because that sounds better than $20,000. But most clients are pretty savvy. They know about how much they should expect to pay. So, in my experience, it's better to quote by the project. Then you can find all sorts of creative ways to get the project done faster and easier (such as outsourcing parts of it).

In the end, it's up to you. I find many freelancers start their careers charging by the hour and then eventually move to the per-project model. You're the boss, though. You decide where to start.

You also decide how much you will charge. It's common for people to start at the lower end of the pay scale when they're just starting out on their own. If you're completely new to this work, that's fine. Just realize that you can have a raise anytime you want. You're the boss. Take into consideration how long you've been doing this kind of work. Do you have an advanced degree in your field? Do your clients just *love* you? Do you have more work than you can handle? It might be time to raise your rates.

Whenever you're quoting a price for a project, keep in mind how much value the client gets from the final result. Back when I was copywriting for a living, I was talking with a client about a fairly big job. It was a sales letter that would sell six-figure software. In other words, just one sale from my words would bring that company over $100,000. I was already booked with work and didn't really need this client. So, when the question of price came around, I quoted the highest price I had heard other copywriters charge—$10,000. At the time, that fee seemed like a dream. I had never charged more than $1,000 before. But I was confident I could do an amazing job.

The client agreed. They didn't even question the rate. And that's when I learned that not everyone is trying to find the lowest price! In fact, some of the best clients won't take you seriously if you are too cheap. They'll think you don't know what you're doing.

TAKE ACTION

Do some research and find the range of fees people in your field are charging. Start where you feel your experience and skill merits that fee. But don't wait too long to raise your rates. You're the boss.

Choose Your Clients Carefully

It can be tempting to believe that you need every potential client who comes knocking on your door. This is especially true when you're in a dry spell or you're first starting out. It's not nice to think about, but some people will take advantage of that. They will try to get you to do more work for less money, or even work for free. Others will just be gigantic pains in your backside, even if they are generally nice people and have good intentions.

I've developed a few rules of the road over the last 20 years or so. Each rule has a hard-won lesson attached. Do yourself a favor and skip the hard part. Just pay attention to the rules, and maybe make a few of your own.

Rule #1 > Trust your intuition!

If something feels off or weird or unsettling to you, there's probably a good reason for it. Learn to listen to your gut and trust it. There's no shame in just saying, "No thanks" and walking away.

Rule #2 > Keep a running list of your red flags.

We all have different tolerance levels for BS and drama. It can take years or even decades before some freelancers will turn work down because they know a person might turn into a nightmare client. I'm not trying to scare you here. I just want you to realize you have a choice in who you decide to work for. Over time, you will develop a list of red flags, and you'll get more selective as you go along.

Some red flags to watch out for include:

- Poor communication and follow-up
- Delayed payment
- Scope creep (when the scope of the project expands without additional payment)
- Dishonesty or misrepresentation
- Lack of contracts or agreements of any kind

If you find yourself working for a nightmare client, the best thing you can do is get yourself out of the situation as honorably as you can. The last thing you want is for them to bash you on social media or harass you down the road. Fulfill your obligations if you can, and then simply say you need to terminate the arrangement. Be very careful who you vent your frustrations to. Find a trusted friend and meet them for a coffee when you need to rant a bit. Keep all that off of social media. Be professional…stay classy.

Rule #3 > Avoid possible scams.

For a long time, remote working was uncommon. Working at home was a dream that scammers advertised. Jobs such as envelope stuffing and product assembly were advertised as ways for homebound people to make some extra money. Scammers today are a bit more sophisticated, and even careful job seekers can get caught up in their webs of deceit. So, keep your senses sharp, and if you feel something is amiss, walk away. There are always other jobs. Don't feel as if you must land any one particular offer.

Here are some red flags to watch out for:

- Companies you've never heard of reaching out to you
- High pay for simple work that could be outsourced much cheaper

- Hiring managers or clients who will only talk via chat or text, never in person
- Fake URLs that sound familiar but lead to questionable (or faux) news sites
- Lack of phone numbers or legit email addresses on the website
- Requirement to pay a small sum of money up front for the promise of a big payoff, especially if they ask to be paid by wire transfer
- Request for your confidential information such as banking details or Social Security number
- Unreasonable demands, such as "You must quit your job immediately."

TAKE ACTION

Take your time and research potential remote employers carefully. Google the company name and the word "scam" or "complaints" and see what comes up. Scammers prey on people in desperate situations, so put yourself in a position of power. No matter how badly you may think you need a new job, there is always time to ask questions and check out every opportunity that comes your way.

SECTION 3:

DOING THE WORK

There Is No Clock

Woo-hoo! You've got your first gig. Now it's time to get some work done. People love the idea of remote working—all that freedom to come and go as you please, and to pick and choose your anywhere, anywhen. The downside is that you can fall into bad habits such as procrastination, where you put the work off repeatedly until you have to finish in a panic.

An equally bad habit is becoming a workaholic. This is especially hard for freelancers who've mastered the art of getting clients, or who create their own products such as books or online courses. They work and work and work and rarely take a break. The work is ever-present. There is never a time when they get it all done. They neglect their health, their family, their friends.

Their anywhere becomes a prison, and their anywhen never stops.

As a remote worker, no one is watching the clock for you. There is no clock. There is only the work. Either it gets done or it doesn't.

Most independent workers I know swing back and forth somewhere between the two extremes of procrastination and overwork. I certainly do. The trick for me is recognizing where I am on the continuum and how long I've been there. Is it time to turn the computer off and spend a few days (or weeks) recharging? Or is it time to buckle down and create some sort of schedule for myself?

There's nothing wrong with a good stretch of hustle, you just don't want to stay there too long or you'll burn out. At some point, your body will shut down and get sick, and you'll have no choice but to take a break.

Finding a natural balance is not as simple as it seems. Depending on your job, you might have naturally slow times followed by predictably hectic times. When I'm ghostwriting a business book, for example, I know I have to be extremely productive during the early weeks to finish a first draft. Then I'll get a break while the client reads over it and makes revisions. Next, there will be a steady period of back and forth until we get a final manuscript we're happy with. I know that's the cycle, and I can expend my energy accordingly.

The goal is to have unbiased self-awareness. You must be able to look at your work habits objectively and adjust them if necessary. What's your natural working rhythm? Are you a morning person or a night owl? Do you prefer to work in bursts of intense effort followed by days (or weeks) of rest? Those traits are actually part of your physiology. It's normal for some people to be early risers and for others to prefer the night hours.

Some people are driven by lists. They love to create a set of tasks and then check them off one by one. If you know you succeed best by working along steadily, that's great! Your best approach will be to look at your deadline and work backward, adding appropriate milestones to your calendar. As you reach the next milestone, check it off and do a little celebration dance. Then start moving toward the next one. You might even have a milestone to check off every day. Whatever keeps you motivated and in forward motion is good.

Others of us are deadline-driven, and lists are just annoying. I perform best under a little pressure. No matter how hard my mother tried to convince me to work a little each day, I always wound up doing my homework the night before it was due. And my grades never suffered.

Sound familiar? If so, you might have been made to feel bad about it. But there's nothing wrong with either approach; they are simply preferences. If you know you're not going to get anything done until right before a deadline, that's okay. You have a couple of choices. Either make sure you always have short deadlines, so you're always in productivity mode. Or stop telling yourself you "should" be working, and just enjoy the downtime.

It might take some time and experience (and maybe an upset client or two) before your body figures out exactly when to switch on the productivity. So, be sure you monitor your time and predict how long a task is going to take. As an independent worker, knowing your own work preferences is important not only for getting the job done, but also for staying happy and sane while you do it.

Another psychological preference to consider is whether you're introverted or extroverted. Each type of person needs different working conditions. Unfortunately, in both traditional jobs and remote work situations, we often get put into the wrong environment. We're miserable and we don't know why.

Introverts: It's a common misperception that introverts are shy or antisocial. The truth is that these types of people gain energy by being alone. Their batteries run dry when they're with other people. That doesn't mean they can't function around others, only that they'll need to be alone at some point to recharge. If you're an introvert working in a busy office, chances are you would give anything for an office with a door or a chance to work from home where it's quiet.

The other thing to understand about introverts is that they process their thoughts and come up with ideas *inside* themselves. They think things over before discussing possible options. They like to read over an agenda before a meeting takes place. Remote working can be a wonderful thing for introverts, because they can take the time they need to process and come up with ideas by themselves. But they can also fall into the trap of remaining isolated and never sharing their ideas. Maybe they have a thought for a new product, but they never tell anyone. They keep it inside, constantly perfecting it in their imagination. What a shame!

Remote-working introverts should expect impromptu client meetings and phone calls with managers that crop up without warning. It's uncommon to have an office protocol where a meeting is called and an agenda sent out. This can be a problem for introverts. They hate to be caught off guard, without a prepared answer.

If that's you, consider how you might "train" your clients and managers. Tell them that since you work from home, you need at least 30 minutes of advance warning before attending a call or a meeting. Ask them to text you a specific time they want to talk and the topic(s) of discussion. That way, you'll have some time to collect your thoughts on the matter. Better yet, set up regular meeting times during the week. Or send out a morning memo with times and talking points.

If you're an introvert, remember that you need some time to be alone and recharge, but don't take so much time that you are completely isolated. Acknowledge that you naturally prefer to process your ideas internally before presenting them to others. If you know this about yourself, you can set up your work environment to keep both you and your clients happy.

Extroverts: These people are recharged by being around others, and lose energy when they're alone. They tend to process their thoughts and feelings out loud. They prefer to speak with others to hash out ideas and work out solutions to problems.

The extroverts are the coworkers who walk into your office just to chat. They use meetings to formulate plans and kick around ideas, not to present finalized solutions.

If you're an extrovert working at home, energy management can be a real issue. You need people around you, interacting with you, in order to do your best work. If you're stuck at home alone, your energy can be quickly depleted. Spend too many days in that state and depression can set in. Your thoughts run races around your head, but not much gets done.

So, get out of the house whenever possible. Find different places to work—coffee shops and bookstores are popular. If you're lucky enough to have a co-working space near you, that might be an ideal solution. Set up lunch dates or phone calls with people to brainstorm and talk about what's going on in your work or daily life.

Realize that there is a spectrum of introvertedness to extrovertedness. And many people fall somewhere in the middle. I am almost exactly in the middle, and find that I can work at home happily for a time. Eventually, though, I get restless and need to get away from my familiar surroundings. You might be somewhere in the middle, too. Or you might travel back and forth between the two. That's perfectly normal, and self-awareness is key to managing your energy and being productive.

Working with Your Opposite

Here's where you're going to have a huge advantage over other remote employees or freelancers. If you know your own preferences—introvert or extrovert, list-checker or deadline-driven—then you have the power to work well with anyone!

Say you're an introvert preparing to talk to a potential client about a huge project that you really want. The first thing you'll want to figure out is whether they are introverted or extroverted. Why? Because you'll be able to approach them the way they naturally prefer.

An introvert might email you to set up a meeting for later in the week and send you a list of questions they have about your experience and credentials. On the other hand, an extrovert is more likely to just pick up the phone and call you out of the blue, expecting to be able to hash out a contract right then and there. Because you're savvy about psychological preferences, you can easily switch hit and give the client exactly what they need and expect.

TAKE ACTION

It takes some practice to pick up on the subtle cues people give off about their personality types. But once you figure it out, it's as if you have this human-interaction superpower that helps you land and impress every client you talk to. One assessment for these qualities is the Myers-Briggs Type Indicator (MBTI) test for psychological preferences. If you'd like to develop this superpower to its full potential, I recommend you study more about MBTI.

Set Expectations on Both Sides

One of the biggest sources of friction between remote workers and managers (or between freelancers and clients) is a lack of effective communication. Signals get crossed. Deadlines get missed. Money is lost. All because expectations were not set at the beginning.

Setting expectations is really pretty easy, you just have to remember to do it. Every time. Every email. Every new piece of work. Every stage in a larger project. All you need is the answers to three questions:

- What is the deliverable?
- When is it needed?
- Can you meet that deadline?

For every project you take on, whether it's designing a piece of software or sending an email, know what you need to deliver and by when. If you don't know, ask! And be specific. Your client might need a design by tomorrow. But is that by first thing in the morning or by the end of the day? Know the exact time. It's critical to avoid misunderstandings. This will save you more headaches and make you more money than you can possibly imagine.

It works the other way, too. Whenever you ask for something from a client, give them the courtesy of setting your expectations. Tell them exactly what you need and when you need it. Then get them to confirm whether they can meet that deadline.

If you or the client can't meet an expectation, that's fine. Just be honest. They may be able to adjust the timeline or break the project down into smaller tasks. Realize that your client or manager has a boss, too. You want them to look like a rock star in front of the CEO or their customers.

Maintain Constant Communication

It's frustrating when you hire someone to do a job and then don't hear from them for days or weeks at a time. People get nervous when you just disappear on them. Even if you're working along on the project and doing a great job, if you're not in communication with the client...well, they don't really know what you're doing. For all they know, you took a vacation or died in a plane crash.

Don't leave them hanging. Give them regular updates (at least once a week) to let them know how you're progressing. This doesn't have to take a long time. In fact, you could put together a template to fill in once a week. Your client or manager doesn't need to hear all the little details; they just want to know you're progressing on the project. Your weekly update could be as simple as:

- Project name
- Completed items from last week
- Projected items to be completed this week

When you proactively communicate your progress, your clients know they can trust you. They see that you're working and that you care about the goals and deadlines. Building trust in that way pays off in the long run. On those rare occasions when you can't meet a deadline, clients are often happy to make allowances and accommodate you if you've been in communication the whole time. They are also more likely to remember you and refer you when their friends need the services you provide.

Different clients will want to communicate in different ways. I have some who prefer email, others who like to text, and several who use apps like Voxer, which records audio. I try to avoid long meetings whenever possible, and providing regular updates helps. Sometimes clients want to communicate via group meetings, and that's fine. Zoom is great for video meetings.

Project management software is another great way to stay in touch and show your progress to clients. This type of program helps keep your priorities and deadlines straight, so you don't fall behind or forget about important tasks. There are plenty of programs out there—Trello, Basecamp, and Asana are good ones. Many of them have free versions that are perfect for freelancers. You can create an account, then add your projects, tasks, and deadlines. Projects can be shared with the client and other team members. That way, they can just log in and see where you are, add comments, and generally have input into the project as you're working on it.

This software does not, however, replace the need for weekly updates. Don't assume the client will log in and check your progress. Just give them the option. And keep sending those updates!

Besides deadlines and project details, set expectations about when people can contact you. Even if your work hours fluctuate, set certain hours when clients can call or text you. If you don't, you may find yourself answering texts at 4 a.m. Your mental health is at stake here, and it's easier to set expectations in the beginning. Let them know how they can contact you, when they can expect an answer, and what *exactly* constitutes an emergency. Yes, sometimes that early morning text is critical, so make sure you and your clients know what you consider critical.

TAKE ACTION

Write down some ground rules for your future clients. How and when can they contact you? If they don't reach you right away, how soon should they expect a reply? How will you keep them up-to-date on their projects? Create some type of document (a Welcome Email or PDF, for example) with all this information, including your phone number and preferred email. Then give this to all your new clients when you begin the first project.

Plan for Chaos

One of my mentors, Sean D'Souza, teaches the Chaos Planning System. The idea is that no matter how well you plan your schedule, something is likely going to come along and mess it up. You'll get sick, or another client will have an urgent need, or the most beautiful day will show up and you'll just have to go to the beach!

If you plan for this kind of chaos to disrupt your schedule, then it isn't really chaos at all. It's just life. Your wonderful, amazing life.

How do you plan for chaos? You simply allow for it. Assume that it WILL happen. As a writer, my schedule requires me to draft at least 1,000 new words every day for my current book. There are two ways I could have looked at this. I could have said, "I HAVE TO write a thousand words every single day." That's a great goal, but when I had a chaotic day and didn't get around to it, I would have failed.

Instead, I said, "I need to write at least seven thousand words a week." That gave me much more freedom. I could write 5,000 words in one day, then slow down to 500 words for the rest of the week. If I knew I was going to take a day off, I could move that task earlier or later in the week. As long as I got those 7,000 words within the week, I was good. I was successful.

You can divide up your work however you like. Maybe you establish benchmarks at 25%, 50%, and 75% of project completion. As long as your project reaches those benchmarks by the day you choose, all is well. Even if you barely make it by the skin of your teeth. It's also a good idea to plan for whatever else might go wrong like clients failing to give timely feedback, your computer crashing, or a family emergency.

The beauty of working anywhere, anywhen is the ability to control your own schedule. So, plan for chaos and you'll never feel like you're falling behind. You've got wiggle room.

Speaking of chaos—did I mention you should BACK UP YOUR WORK! (I did? Just thought I'd mention it again.) Nothing will throw your life into chaos faster than losing weeks or months of work. Make sure you back up your computer regularly (daily, if possible) and store that backup data in several different places. Or save yourself time and headaches by having your documents backed up automatically to the cloud.

TAKE ACTION

How are you currently scheduling your time? Write down a few ways you could rearrange your schedule to allow for some chaos now and then. Start planning for at least one day a week to be a total washout, and make sure you're set up to have a successful week in spite of that possibility.

Log Your Work

Some freelance clients will want to see a log of completed work, especially if you're charging hourly. Remote employers will definitely want some record of what you're accomplishing each week. Even if they only want the final product and don't care how many hours you spent on it, logging your work gives you a chance to see how long it *really* takes to complete a task. It shows you how many phone calls you're actually making per day or per week. This information will help you adjust your rates in the future.

If you're a fast worker, charging by the hour might be hurting your income. Instead, you could be charging by the project and getting more money overall. If it takes longer than you thought it would to complete an assignment, you need to know that, too. Maybe there are processes you need to learn better. Maybe there are shortcuts you need to adopt. Or maybe you just need to adjust your expectations (and your clients') about how long it takes to get something done.

Logging your work also helps you prove what you've done if a client decides to bail on you and requests a refund. It helps with bookkeeping and taxes. And it helps you keep track of your income goals.

You can log your work by hand or use a spreadsheet or time-tracking software such as Toggl or OfficeTime. It doesn't matter how you keep track of your work, only that you do it.

TAKE ACTION

If you don't already have a system in place to log your work, take some time to make a simple spreadsheet. All you really need to keep track of is the client, the date the work was done, what was done, and how long you worked on it. This isn't book-keeping; it's just tracking your hours.

Set Boundaries: Working with Kids (or Anyone Else) in the House

The whole reason I started freelance writing nearly 30 years ago was so I could stay home and raise my children. I remember being nine months pregnant with my first and thinking how great it would be if I could work at home. She would nap and play, and I would calmly work sitting next to her. It all seemed so easy in my head.

But if you've ever tried to type with an infant (or a cat) on your lap, you know it's quite a challenge. If you've ever tried to get anything done while caring for a preschooler, you know it's nearly impossible.

So, I had to include this section for anyone contemplating working at home with others in the house. It doesn't matter whether those others are children, pets, roommates, or a spouse who also works at home. You've got to know what to expect, and be prepared.

Set some ground rules, but be willing to show flexibility. Others in the house need to know that when you're on your computer, you're working. Even if it looks like you're just screwing around on Facebook. (It's called research...hello!) They need to know this is not a hobby. It's not a lark. It's your job, and you need to concentrate in order to do it well.

If you're a new mom, the baby comes first. And you're probably going to have to work around a sleep schedule. You might have a rule such as "When the baby is asleep, I'm working." Or you might set certain hours when you work and your spouse takes care of the baby.

If your children are older or you just have roommates, you could make a Do Not Disturb sign for your door. Or let them know that when you're on the computer, you wish to be left alone. Sometimes you can set up subtle cues to let people know you're busy by wearing headphones or ear buds, even if you don't listen to music while you work. Or by closing your office door. Or by setting certain work hours.

When my kids were little, they knew that when Mommy's door was closed, she was working. They mostly understood and tried to follow the rule. Now that they're adults, I actually miss them barging in to show me a picture they drew or to give me a hug.

Rules are great, just don't expect them to be followed all the time. The whole joy of working at home is having the freedom to work when you want, where you want. So, go ahead and take the kids to the park.

Set expectations with those around you. You might have a different schedule from week to week, so let the people in your life know that. If you know the next 10 days are going to be super busy, prepare your spouse. Just don't be "super busy" all the time. Let them know when you have more free time, too. As long as your loved ones know what to expect, your relationships will go a lot smoother.

Remember to give instructions for emergencies. You don't want your house burning down because your kids were following the rule "Don't bother Daddy when the door is closed." Make sure the children know it's okay to break the rule if someone is hurt or something bad is happening.

Don't ignore your kids or set them up with an electronic babysitter (TV, video games, iPad) all the time. There will be times when it's appropriate, but too much of that isn't healthy.

Get creative with your solutions. Is there a park nearby where they can play while you work on a picnic table? Can you trade babysitting time with another work-at-home parent? Could you hire an older child to read or play with your kids? That can be a cheaper solution than hiring a nanny, and you're still in the house if something goes wrong.

Provide plenty of uninterrupted time with your kids. When mine were growing up, I drove them to school and picked them up every day. Those few minutes in the car were so precious. It was a time when they could talk to me uninterrupted. It might not seem like much, but it's valuable time. If you choose to try this strategy, you will get the chance to meet your child's friends and teachers, too. It's pretty cool to feel like part of what's going on at school every day.

Once your kids are older, it's time for them to pitch in and help! Assign chores and expect them to contribute to the family. Once they can drive, have them buy groceries and run other errands so you have more time to work.

Finally, if you have a spouse who works outside the home, make sure they understand what you do all day. It's so easy for them to think you sit home and play or relax. But you are working just like they are. And it's just possible that you won't have dinner on the table every night when they get home.

Working with others around you can be a challenge or it can be a blessing. Setting expectations and keeping in constant communication is the difference.

TAKE ACTION

Write down some ground rules to help your family and friends understand when you're working and shouldn't be disturbed. Remember, if a particular rule doesn't work out the way you thought, you can always revise it.

Set Up Future Work

As you're working on your current projects, you should be setting yourself up for future work. The easiest way to get additional work is through clients you already have. So, remember that as you're working on their project. Staying in regular communication and doing great work goes a long way, but there's more you can do.

Appreciate your clients. Tell them you're enjoying the work. Thank them for giving you the opportunity to help them reach their goals. Send them a handwritten note with a gift card to their favorite coffee shop. People love to feel appreciated, and most of us don't hear words of appreciation nearly enough. It only takes a few words to win yourself a client for life.

Ask for more work when the current project ends. Eventually, every project comes to an end. Even if you're a remote employee, whatever you're working on can eventually dry up. When you can see that you're in the "winding down" portion of the project, start planting the idea that you'd like to keep working for that client. Ask them if there are other projects you might be able to help with. If they say no, ask if there are other departments in the company that might need your services.

Suggest ancillary projects yourself. Sometimes a client gets so wrapped up in their day-to-day work, they don't see things the way you do. As an outside contractor, you have a unique perspective and can sometimes see that a new social media campaign would dovetail with their current initiative quite nicely. If you can imagine a new project that will help them meet their goals, don't be shy about speaking up. For example, when I'm ghostwriting books for clients, I will sometimes suggest that I take over the publishing work or write the marketing materials for the book. Many of my authors have no idea that they need a separate website or video trailer for their books. So, if I wait for them to think of it, I'm out of work. But if I mention some ideas to help them sell more books, they're usually thrilled to have me stay on. After all, who knows the book better than me?

Ask for referrals. If you've been doing great work, meeting deadlines, and showing appreciation, your clients will be happy to refer you to their friends and colleagues. So many freelancers and business owners don't even think to ask for more work. They finish a project and then start looking for new clients. Don't waste this golden opportunity to move seamlessly from one job to the next.

TAKE ACTION

Get yourself some nice note cards and send at least one per week. Create a habit of thanking your past clients for the opportunities they've given you. If you run out of clients, send notes to friends or family. Let someone know you're thinking about them. Just a few sentences on a piece of paper can make a huge difference to your business. It might not seem like a big deal. But when was the last time you received a letter or card in the mail? People appreciate the gesture, and they'll remember you the next time they need your services.

SECTION 4:

GETTING PAID

Collect Your Paycheck

People get wound up in different ways when it comes to money. They're afraid to charge for a project because they're new. Or they're happy to work first and then get paid afterward because they want to prove themselves. Some people work on a handshake, others go with detailed contracts. Some charge by the hour, others charge by the project.

Here's the thing—we all have our own comfort levels with money and agreements. My personal belief is that it doesn't matter how you decide to collect payment for your services, only that you do. The whole reason you're working at all is to collect the money you need to live the life you choose, right?

So, the important thing is that you know how much you're being paid and when. For me, I like working on a handshake for smaller projects. For the most part, it's been fine. I've never had anyone stiff me completely, and there has only been one time where I had to track down the money I was owed. That being said, I usually require at least 50% of my fee up front before I start any work at all. Then the remaining 50% is due halfway through the project. For any amount under $1,000, I collect the entire fee up front.

This requires a level of trust on the client's part. They have to feel confident that they'll get the work they're paying for. Sometimes a potential client will say something like, "How do I know you'll deliver high-quality work?" or "What if I don't like what you write?" I used to try to justify myself in these situations. Now, I just tell them to look at my work samples, read my testimonials from other clients, and make a decision.

If they aren't confident I can do the job, I really don't want them as a client anyway. Problems will likely crop up down the road. When I started adopting the mindset that I didn't *need* any job that came my way, life got so much easier. I chose myself. I know I'm capable of doing any gig that comes my way. But if the client hesitates, then I don't have to work with them.

Now, handshake agreements don't work for everyone. If you feel more comfortable with a contract in hand before you start work, by all means you should do that! Make sure you have one set up and ready to go. I'm not a lawyer, and I don't play one on TV. So, I'm not going to give you legal advice about creating contracts. But in general, the more money that's at stake, the more you need a written agreement. Even a simple email detailing what both parties agree to is better than nothing.

You can find sample contracts and agreements through industry associations, unions, and websites. For freelance writers, the National Writers Union provides some good templates. You could also hire a lawyer to help you create a template that protects your rights. If you have a standard agreement, don't be afraid to negotiate the terms. Each client is different, and they may feel strongly about certain points.

At a minimum, your agreement should cover the following points:

- Specific tasks you will and will not complete
- Deliverables you will provide (and by when)
- Resources the client is expected to provide (and by when)
- Cost for the project
- Due dates and payment methods

- Consequences (for both parties) if part of the agreement is broken
- Clause indicating that "payment of the deposit implies agreement with these terms" (or similar)
- Signatures or electronic approval

As you're working on the project, remember to keep a paper trail or a log of your activities. Make sure you can prove what you promised, what they promised, and what you delivered. Hopefully, you will never need to go back to your agreement to solve a dispute. But it's good to cover yourself, just in case.

Somewhere in your verbal or written agreement, you'll want to address possible scope creep. This is when you agree to one set of project parameters, and the client keeps asking for more and more. The scope of the project creeps up and up, sometimes without the expectation of additional payment.

It's a good idea to outline the exact scope of the project, so that you are justified in saying, "Sure, Mrs. Client, I will be happy to add on those extra pages to your website. As this is outside the scope of the project, the additional fee will be $X," at which point the client will either agree to the additional fee or back down on the extra work. Either way, you win.

How do you prefer to receive the money? If you're a remote employee, you'll probably have a regular paycheck deposited directly to your bank. If you're freelancing, you might get paid through an online job directory such as Upwork. Or you might need to send out invoices. The easiest way to create an invoice is through an accounting app such as QuickBooks, Wave, or FreshBooks. Some apps will collect payment via credit card with just a click of a link on the invoice. Other times, clients will want to send you a paper check.

I actually prefer checks for larger invoices because the credit card fees on tens of thousands of dollars can be pretty steep. It's easier for me to just wait a few days and deposit the check myself. If it's a client I've worked with before, I usually start working as soon as I send the invoice. For new clients, though, I wait until the check clears before I start working.

Allocate Your Paycheck

When you work for an employer, major portions of your paycheck are allocated for you. In the United States, your taxes, social security, Medicare, and other payments are withheld automatically. But when you're working for yourself, you get to decide when, where, and how much you will set aside. (Note that residents of the US are expected to pay estimated taxes quarterly for both federal and state.)

You're going to need to take care of self-employment taxes, healthcare, and other fees that employees don't.

If you're invoicing clients, don't forget to put some money aside to pay taxes. I know it's tempting to put it off, but sooner or later you'll have to pay up. It can be a rude awakening the first time you see just how much it costs. Check with an accountant to make sure you're taking all the deductions and getting all the tax advantages you can.

Be frugal, especially at first. More than one super-successful business started out bootstrapping and paying for everyday items with credit cards. While that can work out in the long run, think twice about whether you *really* need that second printer or fancy piece of software. It's easy to get caught up in the idea that if we just had the right course or the right tool, we would be successful. But success comes down to one thing—serving people. You want to make money? Help someone. You want to make a LOT of money? Find a way to help a LOT of people. Technology is fun. Worrying about paying your bills is not. Be smart with your credit.

Finally, once you've achieved a steady income, put some of your money aside into a Screw It Fund. When you have a few thousand dollars tucked away, it's really gratifying to fire that pain-in-the-butt client who's causing you nothing but grief. Or be able to repair your car that decides to die in the middle of winter. Or pay for a special getaway when your best friend decides to get married—in another country!

This fund is just a pile of money to provide peace of mind. So, anytime your circumstances seem overwhelming, or when it feels like there's no way out, you can just say, "Screw it!" And change your situation. Move to another town. Fire the client. Leave the abusive situation. Take the once-in-a-lifetime vacation. It might take a little while to build up this fund. But even putting a tiny bit aside can make you feel more in control of your circumstances. Maybe you'll never need to use it, but it's nice to know the money is there.

TAKE ACTION

Consider setting up a separate bank account for your taxes and a Screw It Fund. You might find it's easier to transfer a small amount of money to each account every time you get paid instead of trying to save money in your general account. Then you can just forget about the money until you truly need it.

Make it Through the Dry Spells

One of the biggest challenges I hear from freelancers and consultants is they feel like they're on a roller coaster. They will spend a lot of time marketing and land a client. Then they'll work really hard for that client and ignore their marketing. So, when that client eventually leaves, there's no one to step into that income gap. They'll have plenty of money for a while, then they'll be strapped and hustling for clients.

I get it. I've been there. Sometimes I still find myself stepping into that trap. Not only is this bad for your bank account, it's bad for morale. It's easy to feel desperate when you're in that dip in the cycle. You'll take on any work you can get just to make sure you have income. That means you might miss a great opportunity to land a bigger, better client.

Marketing consistently is one way to avoid that feast-or-famine roller-coaster ride. Saving money for the slow periods is another. Every business has slow periods and off seasons. Yours is no different. You might find that you're really busy from September through May, and then the work dries up for the summer. Maybe the month of December is just completely dead for you, but January 1, everything picks right back up again. It takes time to figure out when your dry spells will appear. So, when you're starting out, just be aware that this will happen, and save some money to keep you afloat until the tide comes back in.

When there's a lull in work, it's common to blame yourself. Maybe you feel like you were "lucky" to get that last client and you really aren't good enough to do this full-time. Imposter syndrome is a huge challenge for freelancers and entrepreneurs of all kinds. The voices in our heads like to say, *When will everyone figure out I'm a fraud? That I'm not really that good? That they shouldn't hire me?* This kind of negative self-talk can really hurt your career. And it's more common than you might think.

If you find yourself thinking this way, try this exercise. List out all the evidence that proves you're *not* a fraud. That you *do* know what you're doing. And that clients are lucky to have you. Your list might look something like this.

- Client X gave me a glowing testimonial.
- Client Y loved my work.
- Client Z is considering a monthly retainer in the fall.
- I have been working in this field for five years.
- I have six months' experience working for clients in my field.
- I have a degree in a related field.

Keep writing until your brain is convinced that you do know what you're doing. That you have gotten clients in the past, and you will do so again. (If you haven't landed a client yet, you can still use this exercise with all the experience and knowledge you currently have.)

You may need to do this exercise more than once. The human brain is wired to default to the familiar. If negative thinking is common, your brain will go back there again and again. You have to retrain it to think positively. You can do it. I believe in you!

TAKE ACTION

If you already know when your slow periods typically occur, write a reminder on your calendar a month or so ahead of time. Seeing that little note can go a long way to relieving any anxiety you might have. "Don't worry, but the dry spell is coming soon. It's normal. Put some money aside now."

Give Yourself a Raise

As a freelancer or entrepreneur, there is no company-imposed ceiling on what you can make. You can make as much money as you want. Remote working for an employer can be a little trickier, but you can still give yourself a raise by creatively finding more ways to serve.

Here's the key:

- If you want to make more, serve more.
- If you want to make a LOT more, serve a LOT more.

The simplest way to do this is by providing more value to the clients you already have. You can keep learning new skills and offer those as additional benefits to your clients or employer. Additional benefits mean higher rates. They will understand that. You can also package your skills together and charge more.

If you're currently writing articles for a client's blog, they still have to format your words, add some pictures, and get it set up on their website. All that takes time. They may be willing to pay you more for a complete content package with the writing, graphic design, and uploading all done for them. Think about what your client needs before and after your particular service or product. How can you provide that to them as well?

Another way to give yourself a raise is to leverage your work. That means instead of providing one project for one client, consider reselling your work to many different people. If you're a photographer, maybe you could bundle your photos together by theme and sell them through stock photo sites, or even on your own website. If you're a project manager, maybe you could collect your favorite checklists, timelines, cheat sheets, and templates for a particular system you have and sell that as a package.

One of the best ways to make more money is to create multiple income streams. Research shows that millionaires tend to have 7–10 different streams of income, which could include salary, courses or products, investments, consulting gigs, books, and speaking engagements.

Perhaps you could teach others what you know through classes, workshops, and online courses. Maybe you could write a book or teach at a local college. Could you do more than one type of freelancing? Could you outsource certain types of work and resell it at a higher rate?

Eventually, you're going to get so good at serving clients that you run out of time in the day to work. When this happens, it's easy to feel stuck at a certain income level. If all your working hours are filled with clients, and you're busier than you'd like to be, it's time to raise your rates. If you're charging $30 an hour, you might move to $50 or $100 an hour. Or more. Perhaps it's time to start charging by the project instead. *You* decide how much you get paid. No one is going to come along and tap you with a magic wand saying, "Okay, now you're worth an extra $2 an hour." You're worth it when you *decide* you're worth it!

The natural resistance to raising your rates is a fear that you'll lose your current clients and you won't find new ones who will pay the new rate. In reality, though, if you're good at what you do and your clients love you, most of them will stick with you. It's human nature to stay with the familiar, even if it costs a little more.

And the new clients are out there, I promise. You might need to change your marketing strategy a bit to reflect your new rates, maybe start fishing in a higher-level pond. But in my experience, for every client willing to pay $50, there are plenty willing to pay $5,000. You simply need the confidence to ask that much and the excellent work to back it up.

TAKE ACTION

Even if you're just starting out, start brainstorming ways you can give yourself a raise as soon as possible. Most of us wait far too long before putting our own needs first. Write down 5 ways you could enhance your current offerings. Then write down 10 different ways you could add another revenue stream to your overall income. Then pick one idea to act on right away.

SECTION 5:

ENJOYING GREATER SUCCESS

Build Confidence

When you're working for yourself, especially if you're selling services to clients, confidence is the name of the game. You need confidence that you will get the work done on time. You need confidence that you can attract and sell clients on your services. Sometimes you need it just to get up in the morning. Confidence is like inspiration—it can disappear without a trace. When that happens, the show must go on. So, sometimes you have to fake it—appear confident even if you don't feel it at the time.

Fortunately, confidence is like a flabby muscle. It might start out weak, but you can develop it over time. The more you use it, the stronger it gets. I wish I could tell you that eventually you'll feel 100% confident all the time. But after more than 25 years, there are still times the doubt and worry creep into my mind. Thoughts such as *What am I doing?* and *Who do I think I'm fooling?* subtly erode my confidence that's been built over all those years.

I think that's just part of being alive, growing, and expanding. You'll get a handle on one part of your job, then you'll want more. So, you'll expand into the next thing. And as you start expanding, it's natural to feel a little hesitant or even flat-out terrified. It's not always pleasant, but it is normal. So, just take a deep breath and start building up the muscle in that new area. Here are a few strategies you can use to build confidence and keep those negative thoughts at bay.

Give yourself permission to start small, if you want.

It's okay to work part-time. It's okay to charge a little less when you're starting out. You don't have to quit your regular job and dive in without a life jacket. You don't build ginormous biceps by spending one badass day in the gym—that'll just land you in the hospital! You build those guns by increasing the demand a little at a time, over the course of weeks, months, and years. Small, consistent increases in demand—that's the ticket.

Fail forward.

You're going to fail. It's inevitable. You're going to struggle sometimes. You're going to hear "No." And that's okay. Every NO gets you closer to a YES. The more and the faster you fail, the closer you get to success. Thomas Edison failed to create the lightbulb thousands of times, but he wouldn't give up until he turned night into day. Imagine how many of his friends and family thought him foolish. Thank goodness he didn't listen to them. Failure just means there's another way you haven't tried. Keep going.

Believe the good and question the bad.

There's feedback and then there's just plain mean-spirited comments. It's so easy to lose all perspective when it comes to feedback. You'll hear 10,000 good things about your work, but for some reason only pay attention to the one or two negative comments. I don't know why, but we humans tend to blow the negative stuff way out of proportion.

When people pay you a compliment, believe them. Accept it as truth. You're amazing! When you hear something negative, question it. Is there something you can improve? If so, great. Is the comment legit? Do better next time. If there's nothing you can do, or someone is just being a jerk, ignore it. Don't engage.

That's a lot easier said than done, I know. Mean comments still sting like a bitch. And the internet makes it so easy for people to say horrible things. Just try not to let it get you down too long. Give yourself an hour or a day to feel upset, then take a deep breath and get on with your work.

Keep a Happy File.

Somewhere on your computer or in a drawer, make a file and stuff it full of all the praise you receive. The emails that make you smile. The social media posts that talk about your mad skills. Your testimonials and case studies. Save them, read them…often. Your confidence will build up one email at a time. Consider putting up a bulletin board over your desk, printing out all the good stuff, and pinning them up where you can see them every day.

You can even start building your Happy File with comments you write yourself. "You are a badass freelancer!" or "Wow, I'm so impressed by how quickly you finished this project." When you're down, reading through every comment will get you feeling better in no time.

Practice good posture.

Did you know your posture affects your confidence? It does. When you stand proud and tall, your self-esteem gets a boost. Amy Cuddy, a researcher at Harvard University, studied the impact of body language on your hormones. She found that open and relaxed postures positively influence testosterone and lower the stress hormone cortisol. In fact, standing for two minutes in what she calls "power poses" can seriously boost your confidence.

Try standing like Superman or Wonder Woman with your hands defiantly on your hips, your chest high and open, chin up, and feet firmly on the ground. Guess what? You start to feel super! Try it the next time you have a meeting with a potential client. Breathing deeply and habitually smiling (even when you have no particular reason to) can also help keep those positive hormones flowing through your body. A certain percentage of confidence is actually chemical, so learn how to activate those chemicals whenever you want.

Surround yourself with people who believe in you.

This is so important. Build a support system you can call on for reinforcement when you have a bad day or shared excitement when you have a good day. Are there other entrepreneurs in your neighborhood? Do you have a favorite online forum where people are supportive and helpful? Does your mom believe in you no matter what?

There are always going to be times when even you don't believe in yourself. When that happens…I'm here. Seriously. I believe in you. No matter what you're trying to achieve, keep working at it. You'll get there. I believe in you.

Now that you know you'll always have someone in your corner, go be that person for someone else. Nothing boosts your self-esteem and confidence like helping others reach their goals. Find a friend or colleague who's struggling to achieve something awesome and buy them a coffee. Send them a card. Or just text and say, "Hey! I believe in you!"

It makes a difference. Believe me.

Manage Time
(So You Can Have More Fun)

Here's the funny thing about working anywhere, anywhen—you tend to work way more than you would in a conventional job. There's a joke: "Entrepreneurs will work eighty hours a week just to avoid going to a job for forty." (It would be funny if it weren't true.)

Entrepreneurs, freelancers, and remote workers often love what they're doing, so working more than 40 hours a week isn't a problem for them. Until it is. If you want to bypass that overworking trap, think about what you're trying to achieve and how many hours you *really* need to work? How much money do you *truly* need to bring in? How much freedom are you *actually* buying yourself?

It's not a big deal if you're totally focused on getting your new business off the ground. It's fine to work around the clock to get a new piece of software working for a client. It's *not* fine, however, if your health starts to deteriorate. It's *not* fine if your family doesn't remember what you look like. It's *not* fine if your friends stop inviting you to hang out.

Sometimes it takes a while to get out of the 9–5 mindset. So many of us believe deep down that we have to work hard to deserve success. We've been taught that we have to earn our money with the sweat of our brows, and that rewards come to those who suffer. That might have been true in the nineteenth or early twentieth centuries when most people worked in factories for an hourly wage. But today we have options. We get to make choices about working harder or working smarter.

You're the boss! You decide how many hours you need to work each day. You decide how much money you need to make each month. Want more free time? You could start charging more for your services, cut expenses, or set up some passive income streams. The point is that you do have a choice. If you find yourself sleeping at your desk surrounded by a mountain of empty pizza boxes, maybe it's time to reevaluate what you're doing and why.

The easiest way to recapture time for yourself and your family is to become more productive. When you're able to get more accomplished in less time, suddenly you have options. You can either work more and make more money…or take more time off. You can roll your eyes and yawn if you want to, but productivity hacking and time management are the keys to your freedom.

Here are several ways I've found that work well to keep me productive and on schedule, with plenty of time for goofing off on a video game or taking a walk on the beach. Or, you know, doing the laundry. (Ha! Just kidding.)

Improve your communication skills.

The better you communicate expectations and deadlines with your clients or managers, the more easily you can schedule your days and weeks. Scheduling is incredibly important when you could theoretically work 24/7/365 and never reach the end of your to-do list. The simplest way to improve communication is to add two words to every email or phone conversation. For every task, clarify exactly what needs to be done and ask, "By when?" If the deadline doesn't jibe with what's already on your calendar, let them know that! Clients and managers tend to get tunnel vision on the task *they* are currently focused on. Once they assign a task to you, it's done as far as they're concerned. So, they move on. But you still have to complete whatever they assigned.

This is a classic miscommunication that happens in offices all the time. But it's even worse when you're working anywhere, anywhen. In order to make the latest deadline, you'll make deals with yourself like, *Well, I still have to finish the graphics for the last website. If I wake up at 2:30 a.m., I'll be able to get those done and get started on the next deadline before the client wakes up.* Nonsense!

Buy a calendar or project management software such as Basecamp, Asana, or Trello and make a schedule the client can see. Schedule out your assignments, allowing plenty of downtime. Then, if a client gives you something new to do that you know you won't be able to get to for a week, you can say, "Would you prefer that I work on this assignment or the last one you gave me?"

Very often, they won't even realize how fast they are delegating work. Don't be afraid to let them know you have a schedule to stick to. If the time is blocked off on your schedule—whether it's for another task, another client, or a soccer game—it's blocked off!

Sometimes there won't be any problem pushing the date back to a more reasonable deadline. Sometimes the client will want to know why it's taking so long. Tell them if they want priority on your schedule, they can set up a monthly retainer to hold their spot. Just make sure they know that retainer must be paid whether they give you work or not, and your schedule still applies.

If you become overloaded with work, try outsourcing some of it to a team of your own. Or raise your fees so you don't need to take on quite so many clients.

Remove decisions from your day.

Every decision you have to make during the day costs you energy—from what to wear to what to make for supper. The fewer decisions you have to make, the more energy you'll have to focus on work. The more focused you are on your work, the faster it will get done.

Some people go so far as to wear the same outfit every day of the week. They never have to choose what to wear. They have seven pairs of jeans, seven red t-shirts, and seven pairs of underwear and socks. Every day is the same. That may seem extreme, but it works for many people who don't set fashion as a high priority. Others eat the same thing every day, or visit the same restaurant on Monday nights. They don't have to make a decision about what to eat. Keeping a schedule on a calendar is another way to remove decisions. You know exactly what you're supposed to do each morning, afternoon, and evening. There's no guesswork.

You may feel as if this takes away the very freedom you seek. If so, find ways to remove decisions elsewhere. Can you set up a menu for the week so you know exactly what to buy at the market and what to start cooking at supper time? (My own life runs much smoother when I do this. I save money and my family eats healthier, too.)

Where else can you remove decisions?

- Establish a specific time to check email.
- Set a time and duration for social media.
- Make appointments such as oil changes, checkups, and haircuts on autopilot by scheduling the next appointment when you're wrapping up the last one.
- Assign one afternoon a week to get all your banking and miscellaneous errands done.

The more decision making you can remove from your day, the more you will get done. (And you'll start to feel like a super-organized superhero.)

Remove distractions.

This one is huge. How often are you interrupted by notifications on your phone or computer? How many times an hour do you receive text messages? It's astounding how distracted we've become in this modern world.

One of the hardest things I ever did was to delete my email accounts from my phone. I thought I was saving time by answering email anytime it came in. But I found I was constantly and compulsively checking for new messages. I didn't even realize I was doing it. My hands just clicked the buttons all by themselves, and the next thing I knew I was deleting junk mail, which was certainly not the best use of my time.

Even five minutes here and two minutes there added up to HOURS of wasted time—hours I could have spent with my kids or walking in the woods. And it turns out I only get about 5 to 10 important emails during the day. But 95% of the mail I was responding to was spam. What a waste! So, I got rid of those apps on my phone and stopped the notifications on my laptop. (I'm not quite disciplined enough to check my mail just once a day, but I am getting closer.)

What else distracts you? How many notifications do you have on your phone for social media, text messages, and the like? Turn them off! They are not helping you.

One of the best gifts my mother gave me growing up was not turning on the TV during the day. We just never did it. She wasn't into *Oprah* or the morning shows, so I didn't develop the habit. Now, I love a good Netflix binge-watch session as much as the next girl, but I don't feel the urge to flip the TV on until around 9 p.m.

Do you watch TV during the day? Some people use it as a reward in between work sessions, and there's nothing wrong with that. Just limit how many shows you watch before you get back to work. If your brain really wants to procrastinate, you'll find yourself watching a whole season and then scrambling to reach your deadlines.

Sometimes it's your kids or neighbors who distract you. That's a tricky one. If it's your own children, set rules so they know when you're not to be disturbed. Just don't use work as an excuse to ignore them. If it's the neighbors or other family members dropping by for coffee because they assume you aren't really working, well...you might have to get a little assertive. Tell them you have certain working hours when you need to avoid interruption. Or you could put a Do Not Disturb sign on your door. Maybe escape the house completely and find a secret café they don't know about. To work effectively, you must set boundaries, especially with other stay-at-home parents who don't work while the kids are at school.

Get up early or stay up late.

Sometimes this one can be tough, but it was a blessing in disguise for me. When my kids were little, the only way I could get extended time to myself was to wake up super early. I would rise at 4:30 a.m., make my coffee, and have two glorious hours of time to just write. I soon began to enjoy my private time and got a ton of work done that way.

Once they were all in school, this was no longer necessary. I got my needed quiet time during school hours. So, I slipped out of that habit. The point is that getting up early, for me, wasn't a punishment for not getting my work done the day before. And it wasn't a necessity due to overscheduling myself. It was just a time when I knew I could get work done. So, it worked out well.

If you try this strategy and find yourself ignoring your family or neglecting your health, this might be a negative habit. But it is definitely an option. Just pay attention to how you feel while you're working. If it feels good, and your non-work life isn't suffering, awesome!

Hire a housekeeper.

Seriously. You might think that's a luxury. If you're like every remote worker I know, you will try to work and keep your house clean, and eventually the house will lose. And then your sanity will start to slide as the guilt creeps in over the unwashed dishes and piles of laundry. A housekeeper is not a luxury. Quite often, it's an essential business-building tool. 'Nuff said.

Use time-tracking software.

Sometimes we just need an objective look at where we're really spending our time. There are lots of different tracking software tools you can use to measure exactly how much time you spent on Facebook yesterday…and how much time you spent looking at your email…and how much time you actually worked on client projects. It can be truly eye-opening when you see the numbers. Even if you don't track your time for a boss or client, try using this software once a week or so. Just for fun. If you like what you see, great. If not, you have the power to make changes.

Developing productivity tools and habits is an important part of working anywhere, anywhen. There's no boss lurking around your cubicle to make sure you're getting things done. You're completely capable of managing yourself and your work. And there's no reason to work more hours than you have to. If you can complete a project in two hours, there's no need to work for eight. Be ruthless with your time, and keep as much of it for yourself and your family as you can.

Balance the Workload

When you get to decide *what* you work on, *when* you work, and *where* you work, there's a never-ending stream of tasks to be completed. When there's no work to be done, there's marketing. When there's no marketing, there's bookkeeping and admin tasks. When there's no admin, there's continuing education and networking. When you work for yourself, you're not just doing your job—you're also responsible for every other job in a typical company.

Your workload quite literally never ends...until you say it ends.

So the temptation is always there to keep working. To get up early so you can finish that client's website. To skip breakfast, because you're not really hungry anyway. To keep working on the next client's super-rush emergency project. Lunch? Just microwave some chicken lumps. You'll have a salad for dinner. Wait! A client calls with changes that *must* be made today. It's an emergency (again)! Everything is launching in two hours. So you drop everything and get to work on their needs. You work right through dinner, skip the movie date you had planned, and fall into bed at 2 a.m. with your phone beside you in case something comes up.

That is no way to live!

Yet for many of us, that is a typical day. Then we wake up at 6 a.m. and do it all over again. You have to decide when enough is enough and figure out a system for setting priorities. You may have heard the magic word "systems" before. I heard it for a decade, but dismissed it as too constraining for me. I told myself, "I'm a free spirit. I do what I want, when I want. I've got it all handled."

And I did. Except my life was extremely hectic!

I held it all together on the outside. The kids got to school. The groceries were put away. Dinner got made (usually). And I had a steadily growing business. But inside, I was usually in one of two extremes—overworked and exhausted or out of clients and panicked about where the next paycheck was coming from. I was caught in the classic freelance feast-or-famine cycle. The roller coaster. I needed systems to help me feel in control.

I'm still far from perfect with using systems, but I'm getting there. And one thing I've learned is that *you* get to decide which systems work for you. And if existing ones don't work, you can make up new ones. You're still in charge. Systems simply give you a way to remove some of the decisions you have to make every day.

So, here are some of the systems I've found that work for my own rebellious spirit—the part of me that *hates* being put into a box or a schedule. I consider them more like guidelines or suggestions than actual systems. I can actually handle these loosey-goosey rules and ideas. Maybe they'll work for you, too.

Know your top three priorities for the day.

What's the least amount of work you can get done and still feel as if you did a good job? Every night before you stop working, determine the next day's top three tasks that should be done. Just three. No more, no less. These are your priorities.

For me, they usually look like this:

1. Write content for my current work in progress (WIP) book.

2. Work on client book or campaign.

3. Record podcast interview or write email newsletter.

That's it. That's all I have to think about when I start working in the morning. Once I have my coffee in hand, I start on the first task. Then I take a break and move to task #2. Take another break and move to task #3. By then, it's usually noonish, and I've done pretty much everything I have to do for the day. Of course, sometimes I have more than three things that *must* get done. I don't miss deadlines. But when you run your business with this system, you don't get into those situations as often as if you're trying to wing it.

Now, you might be thinking, *What about client emergencies?* I try not to have them, for the most part. I stay in good communication specifically to avoid those time-wasters. You might also be thinking, *But if you're only working, like, four hours…you could do so much more!* Yes, I could. And often, I do. Usually after dinner. But it's a choice, not a necessity. My current WIP and client work brings in the money. And my podcast is my marketing. Every now and then, I do admin and bookkeeping tasks, but that's really light work.

By removing the decisions about what I'm going to do first, what must get done, and how I'm going to find my future clients and customers, I'm freeing myself from hours of work every day. My work. Client work. Marketing. Done!

Tackle the biggest task first.

When you look at your prioritized list of things to do, what's the one thing you really don't want to do? What's going to take the longest or put you the most outside your comfort zone?

Is it calling a client to give bad news? Do it first! Is it working through a really boring spreadsheet? Get it done! When you tackle the biggest or most dreaded task first thing, you get it out of the way. It's done. And the rest of your day is a piece of cake. Usually, I find that "big deal" item wasn't really all that terrible. And because I just tackled it and got it done, it didn't take as long as I thought it would. Work is funny like that. When I stop building things up in my head and just do them, they become simple. Or at least, they get done.

If you're a list maker with to-do lists a mile long, it's really tempting to do a whole lot of smaller tasks first. Why? Because then you can cross 20 things off the list. But guess what? You probably invented many of those 20 tasks just to avoid the one thing you know you really need to do. If you just call the damn client or work the freakin' spreadsheet, all those other little tasks will either fall by the wayside or get done anyway. Don't put off that big deal task. Do it first. You'll be glad you did.

But what if *everything* is a big deal, everything is urgent? Then you do the thing that is merely important first. For a long time, client work was always the most urgent task for me to complete. After all, they were paying the bills. I was prioritizing urgent, then important, then other stuff. But I discovered I was doing it all wrong. My important items were not getting done because the urgent ones took up all my time. So, I started doing the important items first, and guess what happened? The urgent ones got done. Of course they did— they were truly urgent. They *had* to get done. I didn't have the option to ignore them.

How did that shake out in the end? I got more accomplished because the urgent task was waiting with its looming deadline, and I consciously put it off until the important one was done first. Did I miss urgent deadlines? No. And that's because I didn't always complete the important task. Sometimes, I had to break it into smaller bits and take more days to complete it.

The key is that I made progress on something that I would normally have put off and never gotten done.

Work in blocks.

Have you ever noticed how sometimes you can be working along for hours and time seems to fly by? You're in the zone, concentrating and getting loads of work done very quickly. Wouldn't it be awesome if you could make that happen whenever you want?

Well, you can. You just have to train your brain to do it. Some really smart people have studied the human brain and discovered that focusing on one task in blocks of time is far superior to the old multitasking way of getting things done. There are many theories about which is the best way to block out your time, but the key is to focus on one task at a time.

I use something called the Pomodoro Technique. (Pomodoro means "tomato" in Italian. The guy credited with inventing this strategy used a kitchen timer shaped like a tomato.) With this technique, you set a timer for 25 minutes. While the timer is going, you work on one task. You work as quickly as you can and attempt to complete the task. When the buzzer goes off, you take a short five-minute break. That's one pomodoro. You might have completed your task, or you might still have more to do. Either way is good.

After your break, you set the timer for another 25 minutes. Work on one task. Then take a short break. You are training your brain to turn off all the distractions and focus on getting something accomplished quickly. You're training yourself to get into the zone whenever you desire. Pretty cool, huh?

After about four pomodoros in a row, you'll want to take a longer break. That break could be 30 minutes or several hours. Since you get to work anywhere, anywhen, you may decide to do four pomodoros in the morning and then go for a long lunch. Or maybe you do three pomodoros and then get some exercise. (Note: There are several phone apps to help with pomodoro timing.)

You've got your prioritized list of things to do. You've got your timer. All you have to do is block off an hour or two at a time to get your work done. You'll be amazed at how much you accomplish when you remove the distractions and focus on one task at a time. Suddenly, you'll write faster, you'll code more easily, or you'll design more beautifully than ever before. I don't know why it works. It just does.

Maybe you run two early-morning pomodoros before you go running and take a shower. Maybe you don't get going until noontime, and then you can run six pomodoros in a row without a problem. Maybe you have to schedule around school and sports for your kids.

My usual routine is four pomodoro sessions in the morning between 8 and 10 a.m. I get a good deal of writing done during that time. Then I take a break and get something to eat. I'll also check my email and maybe some social media. Then it's back to work.

During the school year, I usually stop working around 1 p.m. Then I run errands, pick up my kids from school, and get them settled into whatever activities they have going on. Sometimes, I'll even take a nap! ('Cause I'm the boss and I can.) Then, around 4 p.m., I usually work for another hour or so. And if there's a deadline coming up, I'll pick up again around 6 and keep going for an hour or two.

I'm basically working in two-hour blocks, they're just spread out over the entire day. If I wanted to, I could just work six or eight hours straight then take off. But that doesn't seem to work as well with my family's schedule. That's why I love being able to make my own hours.

When you're on a break, no matter the length, actually take a break! Get up and away from your workspace, walk around, do some stretches, and drink some water. We tend to neglect our bodies while we're working (and sometimes the rest of the day, too).

Human beings were not designed to sit in chairs staring at screens for hours on end. You need to move. You need to hydrate. Sometimes I catch myself taking a break by sitting in the same position and switching my screen to Facebook or email. That's not a break. That's distraction! If you need to check email and social media for work, do it during a work block.

Work from your calendar.

Some people love to-do lists. They take pleasure in checking off items and making it all the way to the bottom. It offers a sense of completion. I am not one of those people. When I write a to-do list, it's really just a reminder list. I never actually cross things off. And I never get to the end, because there's always more to do.

In my line of work, I'm *never* finished. Leonardo da Vinci once said, "Art is never finished, only abandoned." When the book deadline hits, I have to be done. Even though I could keep tinkering with it for weeks.

If lists don't really motivate you, here's an alternative I learned from a guy named Kevin Kruse. He wrote a book called *15 Secrets Successful People Know About Time Management*. In the book, he says if a task will take less than five minutes to complete, just do it. Don't think about it, don't add it to a list, just do it.

If it will take longer than five minutes, ask yourself whether it's something you should delegate to someone else. If yes, delegate it. If not, put it on your calendar. Instead of (or in addition to) keeping a to-do list, put the tasks on your calendar with time blocked out. This way, you know exactly when you plan to tackle each one. Remember, every decision you make during the day costs you energy. With this technique, you're taking the decision making out of your day. You simply follow the calendar.

This technique is also brilliant if you have a manager who routinely overloads you with work or who doesn't appreciate how much time an assignment actually takes. In a manager's mind, once a task is assigned, it's as good as done. They often forget that it has to *actually* get done.

When you have a calendar with each task blocked out for the amount of time it's going to take, you have a way to cover yourself. The next time a manager needs something done, and you're already working on the last thing they needed done, just say, "Great! I understand you need this new design finished. So, is it a higher priority than this website you assigned me yesterday? Should I stop working on that one and put this one in its place?" It's amazing how often managers don't realize how much work is really on your schedule.

When you're working with clients, it's a little bit trickier. They believe their work is your highest priority, but it's likely you're working on deliverables for several clients at once. So, you have to be really careful to schedule out the tasks on your calendar and let them know, "Okay, I can schedule that for Thursday." Or "I can get that back to you by the middle of next week."

It's crucial that you set an expected delivery time for every task and every client. Otherwise, you'll overbook yourself trying to please everyone. Eventually, things will fall through the cracks or you'll have a nervous breakdown (or worse).

Use your calendar. It's a wonderful tool.

Build Productive Habits

Do you know anyone who has the discipline to sit down at the same time every day and just do their work? Without drama? Without procrastination? Without one more cup of coffee? We call those people dedicated, disciplined, or just plain freaky. But what they really are is habit-driven.

Similar to how you reach for that first cup of coffee every morning, you can create a habit out of your work. It's a state of mind where the work gets done as quickly and efficiently as possible. Of course, you can also consciously instill a habit such as healthy eating or daily exercise. But this is a book about work, so we'll stick to that one.

If you really want to dig into this topic and all the science behind it, I recommend you read *The Power of Habit* by Charles Duhigg. It's a fascinating look at how habits are created by accident, and how you can create them consciously. Basically, scientists have discovered that habits are just routines our brains run on autopilot. We don't have to think about them. In fact, brain activity decreases significantly while you're in the process of performing a habit. Do you open the refrigerator door every time you walk into the kitchen? Do you think your brain makes a conscious decision to do that every single time? Nope. It knows the automatic pathway: you're in the kitchen, you open the fridge, regardless of whether you're hungry.

It turns out, habits are simply behavior loops. They have a trigger or a cue (something that starts the habitual behavior), a routine (the habit itself), and a reward (the feeling you get that keeps the habit going). Most of our habits are formed unconsciously, so we don't really know what triggers them until we stop to analyze them. Duhigg recommends starting by analyzing your current habit routines. What series of actions are you performing regularly? What's the reward at the end of those actions? And most importantly, what triggers or cues the actions to start?

A trigger is a physical action that sets the routine behavior in motion. My morning routine starts with me walking downstairs and immediately putting the kettle on to start my coffee. This action is automatic. It just happens. While I'm waiting for the water to boil, I put the coffee into my French press and empty the dishwasher from the night before. By that time, the water is ready and I make my coffee. With coffee in hand, I head to wherever my laptop is and I start work for the day. It all happens without any decision making on my part. It's all habits.

A trigger can be anything. It can be turning on a light switch, walking into a room, sitting in a certain chair, putting a child to bed, or even taking a deep breath. Your brain is like a computer: whatever programming you install and keep active, it will retain.

Walk downstairs > put the kettle on

Coffee in hand > open the computer

Open computer > go to email, then Facebook, then look at my priorities for the day

If you want to instill a new habit, you can attach a new trigger to a physical action you're already doing. It's like a daisy chain where one action links to another. Let's say you wanted to start taking a walk in the morning before starting work. You could chain that habit onto finishing your morning coffee. As soon as you rinse out your mug in the sink, you put your walking shoes on and head out the door.

Notice I didn't say that you head out for a 20-minute walk. The goal is to put one *simple, achievable* action after another. Rinse the mug. Put on the shoes. Walk out the door. Once you've done that, you might as well keep walking to the end of the driveway. And once you're at the mailbox, well, you might as well turn up the road and go for a walk. The reward is feeling good about doing something healthy for your body.

Maybe your daisy chain looks like this: you walk into your work room, sit down, take a deep breath, open your computer, set your pomodoro timer for 25 minutes, and start typing. You're off to a productive start to the day. That's the reward— the good feeling that you've started your day right.

Maybe your freelance work starts at the end of the day. Your routine might look like this: you pick your child up from grandma's house, feed him supper, give him a bath, read him a story, kiss him goodnight, walk to your computer, and start working.

Maybe you travel a lot and a habit routine is that you get onto an airplane, you buckle your seatbelt, say hello to your neighbor, and pull out a red folder with notes for your next speech.

Maybe you close your computer for the day, slip on your sneakers, and go for a run.

You're the boss. You can instill whatever habits you want. And you do that by daisy-chaining simple actions that just get you into the zone where it happens without you even thinking about it. Don't get me wrong, it does take time and lots of repetition to make a habit stick. But when you intentionally instill the habits you want, magic happens!

So, think about it. What habits do you wish you had? Write them down, then brainstorm some activities you're already doing that you could chain them onto. Make sure you're trigger-ing something very easy and ridiculously achievable.

Instead of "I'm going to go for a walk every day at four o'clock," say, "When I close my computer for the day, I'll put my sneakers on. And once my sneakers are on, I will walk outside. Once I'm outside, I can just take a little stroll up the driveway."

Once you've achieved the small action, you can always choose to stop. But there's just a tiny next step, so chances are you'll keep going. So, instead of saying, "I'm going to walk for twenty minutes," tell yourself you're just going to stretch your legs a bit and walk for four minutes. You can do that much. It's not a big deal. But once you're moving, you're more likely to go the full 20 minutes. And you'll feel amazing.

Another part of instilling habits is having a positive reward. Your brain loves the feel-good chemicals that flood in when you do something you feel proud of. When you go for a run, endorphins naturally flood your brain. That runner's high is a real chemical reaction.

So often when we finish a good day's work, we fail to reward ourselves. Instead of smiling and feeling a deep sense of pride for moving forward on a project, we despair at how much fur-ther we have to go. We don't even acknowledge how far we've come. Stop that!

I don't care if you work at home or you're in a cubicle work-ing a day job—when you finish work for the day, acknowledge your accomplishments. Smile. Take a deep breath. And tell yourself, "Good job! Wow, you made so much progress. Today was amazing, and tomorrow I'll get even closer to the finish line on this thing."

Don't wait for your boss or clients to reward you. Give yourself this gift every day and your life will change. You want a habit to stick? Give your brain the reward of those pleasure chemicals. Talk nicely to yourself. Tell your brain you appreciate how hard it works for you every day. Love yourself. Appreciate yourself. It's a gift you deserve.

Outsmart Resistance

What about those niggling little thoughts that creep up and keep you from starting work as soon as you have your coffee in hand? Resistance is going to be there, especially at first. Good habits require regular repetition or they won't stick. This is tricky.

When I open my computer, my first inclination is to read my email. And then my old habits kick in and I hit Facebook for a while, then sometimes Pinterest, and then I might go back to email. It's a cycle that can eat up hours if I let it go unchecked.

To beat that habit, I have to leave my writing screen open when I close up for the day. When I get my coffee and open my computer in the morning, I see the work in front of me (not my email). Author Kevin Kruse calls this "beating your future self." It's like time travel. I know my "morning self" is going to be tempted to open email first. So, I outsmart Future Me by leaving the work screen up.

You're outsmarting Future You when you plan a healthy dinner earlier in the day. When you leave your workout clothes lying by your bed, so you put them on and go for a run, instead of putting on a dressy outfit and skipping your workout. See how that works?

Sometimes the resistance isn't a habit, but distracting little thoughts that can derail you for hours—especially if they're deceptively helpful. When I'm writing, I'll sometimes get brilliant new ideas for future books. Or I'll come up with a marketing idea that I really want to share with my client. Or I'll start having doubts about some current project. The doubts are the worst because they can derail a project for weeks, months, or even permanently.

When those resistance thoughts pop into your head, write them down for later. Get the idea or the worry out of your head in one or two sentences, and tell your brain that you can revisit them later. Right now, you're working. And keep your word. Really go back and look at those notes. Sometimes, you'll realize you had a really great new idea. And other times, you'll see it was just a distraction.

If the mental clutter gets really bad, some people wind up with anxiety attacks, or they talk themselves into a frenzy of both good and bad scenarios that might happen. If that sounds familiar, you'll need a strategy to clear your head and get you back on track quickly. There's no boss looking over your shoulder to make sure you get your work done. Mental clutter can completely demolish your ability to work, and that can lead to unpleasant consequences. So, what can you do?

The key is to keep your mind in the present. You might decide to learn meditation techniques and practice them every day. People have used meditation to clear mental clutter and resistance for thousands of years. It takes practice, but it works.

What if you're on a deadline *right now* and you need a quick fix to get your head back in the game? Then it's time to bring your focus to the present moment. Get your brain out of the future or the past, and focus on what is happening in this very instant. One way to do that is to pay attention to your breathing. Take a deep breath in through your nose, and slowly let it out through your mouth. Focus your attention completely on your breath. When you do this for 10 or 20 cycles, your blood chemistry actually changes. Your blood becomes more oxygenated, and you'll feel a lightness come over you. Those distracting thoughts will fade away. They might come back, but you can always repeat the technique anytime you need to.

Another technique is to focus on something in your immediate environment. Look at your cup of tea. Really look at it. Notice the shape, the color, the texture. What cloudy formations appear when you swirl it around? You're letting go of all the mental clutter and completely focusing on one object. Maybe it's a person outside your window. Maybe it's a squirrel on your lawn. It doesn't matter what the object is, just that you spend some time noticing it.

Do not pass judgment on the object. Do not form opinions. For example, I'm looking at my carpet right now. Instead of noticing the color and texture and length and fullness, I'm thinking, *Damn, when was the last time I vacuumed?* That's not helpful. If you find yourself doing that, pick a different object to focus on, and avoid any judgments or stories your brain tries to make up. All you're trying to do is notice what is. Noticing something in the present moment frees you from your thoughts about the past or the future.

Once you're refocused on the present, get back to work. Those thoughts may show up again. That's okay. You have a strategy to deal with them. Try the breathing again. Bring your attention to an object in front of you. Focus on the present moment. And then get back to work. The more often you do this, the better you'll get. And before long, your brain will get the hint. Instead of 10 deep breaths to refocus you, it might only take 3.

Productive habits can take a long time to instill into your everyday life. But it's worth the effort. Carefully craft the habits you want for long-term success, and they will serve you well for years to come.

Stay Healthy

When your mind is focused on bringing in clients and completing projects, it's incredibly easy to ignore your health. This is especially true if you also take care of family members, an aging parent, or even a beloved pet. We all tend to serve others first and put ourselves last. That behavior seems virtuous on the outside, but by neglecting your own health, you're putting those you love at a disadvantage.

If you're too tired to make a healthy dinner, your kids suffer. If you're mentally depleted, you can't have meaningful conversations with your spouse. If you're constantly getting colds or other ailments, you can't be there for your family the way you want to.

It can be challenging to focus on your own health and well-being. Sometimes we look at ourselves and don't like what we see. It's easier to just bury ourselves in work than to take a long look at our health habits and improve them. I get it…believe me.

So, let's start with some small, simple health habits you can start building. Even if you still work in an office every day, these habits will improve your state of mind and state of body. And they'll prepare you for a more productive day, no matter where or when you work.

Get enough sleep!

I love sleeping. I can't imagine not getting a lovely, restorative eight to nine hours a night, and maybe a nice nap in the afternoon. But that's just me. I realize other people feel they're too busy to sleep, don't need as many hours to feel refreshed, or have insomnia and *can't* sleep very well. I'm not a sleep expert, but I do know that if you put your work ahead of your need to recharge, sooner or later you're going to crash. You'll get sick, or you'll just have some sort of physical breakdown that forces you to get the rest you need.

We all have those occasional new-product launches or tight deadlines where we really do need to push through and get some extra work done. Sleep may suffer a bit. But if your work schedule regularly disrupts a good night's sleep, it's time to reevaluate.

- Do you have too much work from one particular client or manager? Maybe it's time to work from your calendar and let them know they are double-booking your time.

- Do you have too many clients? It might be time to raise your rates or cut out the people you don't enjoy working with.

- Are you constantly working on marketing activities because you don't have enough clients to pay your bills? In this case, you might need to switch to more effective marketing.

Sometimes, we use marketing as a stall tactic, too. Is there something you're avoiding, such as talking to prospective clients on the phone? Maybe your marketing "churning" is your way of feeling good about putting that off. Activities such as blogging, fiddling with your website, and constant social media posting *can* be good marketing tools. But they can also be great procrastination tools.

Eat something green every day.

I'm not going to preach to you about diet. But if you're like a lot of remote workers I know and get most of your nutrition through a cereal box, you might want to think about broadening your food horizons a bit. If you enjoy eating out, great! Just try to vary your choices a bit. An all-burger-and-fries diet is not going to help you reach your business goals. Fresh food, as free from chemicals as you can get, at least occasionally. Those choices will go a long way toward keeping you productive and happy.

Get out of the house.

If the sun is shining, just step outside for five minutes and soak up some of those rays. Even just a little sun exposure can improve your mood (and your skin). Right now, I'm typing this section in my car with the warm sun streaming in through the window. It seems odd, I know. But sometimes I just *have* to get out of the house, and my car is warm and quiet. Maybe try working at a local park or your back porch. Fresh air and a change of scenery can do wonders for your mood and your business.

Respect your introvertedness or extrovertedness.

How do you process information and store energy? If you get energized around people, you're an extrovert. If people exhaust you, and you need to be alone to recharge, you're probably an introvert. There's nothing wrong with either tendency, it's just the way your body does things.

So, if you're an introvert, respect that you will need to be alone to recharge. You will probably prefer to have an agenda for meetings, so you can prepare ahead of time. If you know that about yourself, you can set up your workday to respect your body's needs.

Same deal for extroverts. You thrive around people, and you need to have other live bodies in front of you in order to process ideas. You need a sounding board on a regular basis. Set your workday up to accommodate that. Maybe you need to be in a co-working space with other extroverts. Or maybe you schedule a standing lunch date with several of your friends throughout the week.

You might also be a little bit of both. The point is to understand how your body and brain work at their peak, and set up conditions to facilitate maximum efficiency. It's not efficient to put an introvert in a loud meeting that was called on the spur of the moment. Nor is it efficient to expect an extrovert to sit alone and come up with ideas to present later. They *could* work that way, it's just not ideal. Set yourself up for success.

Stay hydrated.

Your body is mostly water. You need hydration to stay alive. If you don't stay hydrated, your productivity suffers. So, drink up! If you don't like water, that's okay. You can drink tea, or flavor your water with fresh lemons or limes. Just be sure that what you're drinking actually hydrates you. Caffeine and alcohol DE-hydrate. So, if you consume lots of either of those, you'll need to make up for it by drinking even more water.

Stay pain-free.

A huge percentage of Americans suffers from ongoing aches and pains. Their backs hurt, their hips are stiff, they have carpal tunnel syndrome. The list goes on and on. Much of this pain stems directly from how they work.

Think about it. How do you currently work? Do you sit at a desk all day? Might that possibly contribute to your lower back and hip pain? Maybe you should think about getting a standing desk (or build one out of a table and a stack of books). Working in odd positions like on your bed or perched sideways on a sofa can really do a number on your body if you repeat it too many days in a row.

Do you spend eight hours or more typing? Maybe you should consider a more ergonomic keyboard, or check out some exercises to help alleviate wrist and finger pain.

Do you get regular headaches? Could it be eye strain from too much screen time? Maybe some new glasses or a blue-blocker on your monitor could help.

Take stock of how your body feels on a day-to-day basis. Then pay attention to how you place your body when you work. Pain sucks. Do whatever you can to stay free of it.

Get some exercise.

I saved this one for last because I know some of you will probably just skip over it. You've heard it all before. In fact, you might be reading this and hearing the teacher's voice from Charlie Brown. Or maybe you're already an exercise fiend and don't need convincing.

Look, how much exercise you get is up to you. We all know it's good for us. We all know it can prolong our lives and help us concentrate better. So, if you already exercise regularly, great! Keep it up!!

If you're like me, and have a hard time sticking with an exercise routine, make an effort to do *something* every few hours. Get up and walk around the house. Put on your favorite song and jump around for three minutes. Take your lunch outside and do some stretches on the grass. You don't have to run a marathon to benefit. Start small and stay consistent. (Believe me, I'm writing this as much for me as for you!)

Remember back in the last chapter when you learned about creating habits? Well, all that applies to health habits, too. Find a physical trigger you're already doing and tack a new habit onto the end of it. When your pomodoro timer goes off, stand up and walk around for your short break. Or when you get ready to answer emails, sip on a nice tall glass of water.

I will if you will!

Build and Maintain
Your Support Structure

It doesn't matter what career path you choose—whether you're a freelance designer, ghostwriter, or medical transcriptionist, or whether you work remotely for an employer—you need a support structure. Actually, *everyone* needs a support structure. The hard part is figuring out what that looks like and how to build it without tearing down your existing life.

What is a support structure? It's your safety net. It's the people, places, habits, mindsets, and activities that keep you going when times are tough. Tough times might mean you've run out of money and there are no clients on the horizon. It might mean you have a really demanding launch schedule. It might mean you're really lonely and just need someone to talk to. Tough times happen to all of us, no matter how successful we become. So, knowing you have rock solid support is critical.

Don't worry, you don't have to have everything in place right away. In fact, most people build their support over years of trial and error. And as you progress along your path, your support structure will change. You'll meet new people. You'll adopt different mindsets. There's no such thing as a "perfect" support system. You just need to have *something* reliable in place.

People

Who are your biggest supporters? Who's got your back no matter what happens? Who won't let you wallow in self-pity for more than a day? Who calls you on your BS? It might be a family member or spouse. It might be your best friend or a member of the clergy. It might even be your child or grandchild.

You need at least one person who believes in you *no matter what*. Because the time will come when you don't believe in yourself. You'll question your actions. You'll want to give up whatever great feat you're trying to accomplish. It happens. It's just part of the journey. So, your support people are your foundation. They keep you from being buried alive in your own self-doubt and fear.

It's great to have lots of people who believe in you, but I'm talking about one or two people you can call in the middle of the night. That friend who will help you snap out of whatever drama you've got going on. Put this person's number in your phone and speed dial them anytime you feel yourself slipping into doubt or spiraling downward. Sometimes just a text with a smiley face from someone is enough to get you back on track. You might even invent a code word that reminds you "Get your shit together and stop freaking out! You've got this!!"

When you're first starting out, it's tempting to bring the other person into the drama and use them to wind yourself up further. Sometimes your subconscious can derail you for days or months with this tactic. Tell your support people that their job is to pull you out of the drama and get you moving forward toward your goal again. The faster they can do that, the better.

You probably have one or more support people in your life already. Tell them how much you appreciate them. And offer to be their support person as well. When you see another person going through the same type of mental gymnastics, it's easier to stop yourself before you get caught up in it. Also, you might figure out some great strategies for talking people down when they're ready to jump off a cliff (hopefully just figuratively!)

Then there are the negative people in your life. The ones who want to drag you down. The ones who don't get what you do, and hate that you've escaped the cubicle hell they feel stuck in. Pay attention to the people you hang around with, and reduce (or eliminate) the amount of time you spend with anyone negative. These people are like vampires who will suck you dry of time and energy. Don't waste either of these precious resources on people who don't make you feel good.

Positive Mindset

Another important part of your support structure is your own mindset. How positive are you? Do you truly believe you can accomplish anything? When a client asks you to do something you've never done, do you say yes and then figure it out? Or do you decline because you're hesitant or unsure?

A positive mindset is critical to your success. If you pay any attention to the world, you'll hear people continually whining and complaining and *wishing* their lives were different. Don't join them. See yourself for what you are—blessed with a great career and a brilliant boss (that's you). Even when you're working 100 hours a week to get a product launched, or you're struggling to find clients, positivity will keep you moving forward instead of running circles in your mind.

There are lots of strategies for keeping a positive mindset. Meditation is one way. If you know how to calm your mind and focus on the present, you're already way ahead of your competition.

Another mindset-strengthening activity is journaling. Sit quietly with your thoughts and a notebook once a day or once a week and write down everything you're grateful for. It could be something small, like an amazing cup of coffee you had that morning. Or it could be something big, such as a new client you just landed. Gratitude has been proven to lift your mood and actually improve your results.

Another journaling exercise is to notice and record your moods during the day. When do you typically feel happy and productive? When do you start to doubt yourself? When can you feel yourself starting to make mistakes? After a while, you will start to see trends emerge. For me, I know for a fact that my brain is more susceptible to self-doubt and negative thoughts after 6 p.m. I'm not sure why, but I notice that in the evenings, voices in my head would say things like, *What are you doing? You can't possibly succeed at this. You should just give up. There's no way this is going to work. Stop now before you embarrass yourself.* Maybe you recognize some of those voices.

Then, in the morning, I always wake up positive and excited to move forward. It's like those voices never even happened. So, now I have a rule. If I start hearing those voices, I look at the clock. If it's after 6 p.m., I ignore them. They can keep talking to me, but I know that in the morning, nothing they've said will matter. So, I just wait it out. I think this happens after six o'clock because I've worked a full day by then, and I'm tired. When I'm tired, I'm more vulnerable to the negativity. At this point, I've had decades of practice dealing with these voices. So, if it's after six (and it always is), I ignore them.

If I hadn't tracked my mindset, I wouldn't have noticed that there was a trend related to the time of day. Your trends may be different. Maybe you're more vulnerable in the morning. Or maybe it's a certain week of the month when you get insecure.

The point is to notice when it's happening. Write it down. And then analyze the trends so you can figure out your own unique rhythm.

I have another telltale sign that I need to ignore the voices in my head. Every creative project I've ever worked on has had a predictable rhythm. I didn't always know it was there, but it's always existed. A project starts with a flurry of excitement. I'm researching or buying materials, visualizing how awesome the final product will be. Then, as I start to work, there inevitably comes a time when I hate it. It's complete crap. No one will ever think this is good. What was I thinking? It was a terrible idea!

Have you ever thought this about a project?

At that point, I have two choices. I can stop working, throw the project away, and start over on something else. Or I can push through and just get it done. Just finish the damn thing. It doesn't matter if I never show it to a living soul, I'm going to complete it. Almost like magic, when I choose to push through and finish, I wind up loving it in the end. It's the weirdest sensation when you *know* something is a piece of crap but you push through anyway, and something miraculous happens to make it beautiful.

It doesn't matter if the project is a book or a dinner party or a piece of knitting. It doesn't matter if it's a one-hour project or a two-year slog. The cycle is always the same. So, guess what? Because I know that about myself, I can use the knowledge as leverage. It takes a lot to make me abandon a project these days. That wasn't always the case. I used to cave in to those voices all the time.

It takes practice and great self-awareness to build your mindset muscle. You can do it. Just be patient with yourself. Start by writing down every time you have a negative or positive thought about your work. Note the time. Note the circumstances surrounding the work. Did your mom call right before the voices appeared in your head? Were you hungry? Did you just get back from an invigorating walk? In time, you'll figure out your own triggers and cycles. Until you do, you've got your support people to help you feel like yourself again.

Everyday Habits

These are also part of your support structure. When things go wrong, or you just don't feel like working, your productive habits will take over and get things done anyway. As a writer, I'm always being asked about where my inspiration comes from. How do I stay motivated to write? The fact is, I don't. Plenty of days come and go where I don't want to do anything more than go sit on the beach, or shop with my girls, or stay in bed and read a book. Because I have an anywhere, anywhen business, I can choose to do any of those things at any time. Most days, though, my habits take over and I get the work done anyway. It's kind of a beautiful thing.

You've already learned how to create good habits. You daisy-chain the new activity onto something that's already habitual. You set tiny, ridiculously achievable goals. And you give yourself some sort of mental reward when you've finished the activity. All that's left is to figure out what kinds of habits you really need hardwired into your support structure. If you're working as a remote employee, you may need to get into the habit of sending weekly reports on Fridays. Or maybe you need to get into the habit of completing two solid hours of work early in the morning before the kids wake up.

If you're a writer like me, it's so reassuring to know that you don't have to wait for a muse to descend and hand you inspiration. Writing is a habit, and it will get done regardless of how you're feeling. You can cultivate that same behavior with coding, web development, customer service—anything you do.

Spend some time daydreaming. If you could magically instill one new habit into your life, which would be most useful? Maybe it's getting some exercise first thing in the morning. Maybe it's turning off the computer at a certain time of night (even if the work isn't done).

Write a wish list of habits you'd like to have. Then realize you *can* have them all, if you really want them. It's easier to instill one new habit at a time, though. So, sort your list into priorities and start with the most important one.

Your Team

At some point in your career, you'll find that you spend a lot of time working on piddly little things that you don't enjoy or aren't particularly good at, or don't directly result in income. Things such as scheduling social media posts for marketing, managing your calendar, setting up meetings, and other administrative tasks that take up so much of your time. When you get to this point, it's time to consider building a team.

That idea was really scary to me for a long time, because I thought it meant I had to hire employees. I didn't want to do that. After all, I hated being an employee. Why would I want to manage them? I honestly thought it was better if I just did everything myself.

Here's the problem with that: I wasted a ton of time doing things such as graphic design for Facebook posts. I'm a writer... I'm *terrible* at design. But still I thought I had to do it myself. So, I would work for an hour trying to create something that would have taken a professional about three minutes. And I was never really happy with what I designed for myself. I just got to the point where I'd say, "Good enough" and move on.

The problem was that I could have been writing during that hour. I make my money writing. I'm good at writing. And I have no business doing graphic design. So, I started hiring people to do small projects on Fiverr.com. For $5 or $10, I could outsource my design tasks and get on with my work.

The first time I did this, I needed a website banner. I had spent hours messing around trying to get something that looked halfway decent and finally decided to give this Fiverr thing a try. If it didn't work, I'd be out five bucks. No big deal. When I saw what came back to me just a few hours later, a feeling of euphoria came over me. It was amazing! I'm sure the guy thought my project was no big deal. It probably took him less than 10 minutes to finish. But to me, it was a miracle. My skin was tingling with excitement. The banner looked great, it only cost me $10, and I didn't have to do it!

After that, I was hooked. I started using the same designer for product covers and social media banners and all sorts of things. I started paying him more, too. Just because I was so grateful to have someone reliable to do the work. I had unwittingly started building my team.

Over the years, I collected my favorite go-to designers, audio editors, voiceover artists, and book cover designers. Whenever I need something done that I know is not in my skill set, I have someone I can outsource to. I have a support structure that keeps me focused on my own work.

Do you realize your clients feel the same way about you? When you deliver a clean piece of code, a beautiful website, or amazing customer service, they are so happy to have someone reliable to handle the stuff they don't want to do (or know how to do). It might be no big deal to you, but it is to them. It's valuable. And hopefully they show you appreciation.

Whether they do or not, *you* should show appreciation to the people on your team. Thank them. Leave them five-star reviews. Send them testimonials they can use to get more work. Or offer them bonuses. (Money is always a great form of appreciation!) Treat them the way you would like your clients to treat you. It doesn't cost you to be nice. And you want reliable people on your team.

Did I hire people who didn't work out? Sure. Were those projects wasted money? I don't think so. It's all a learning process. I should have started building a team of outsourced professionals a lot sooner than I did, but I was scared. What if I hired the wrong person? People told me for *years* that I needed help, that I would make more money if I didn't try to do everything myself. I didn't believe them. I was wrong.

You have the same opportunity right now. Start outsourcing tasks that take up too much of your valuable time—even if it's just to a neighborhood kid. (And by the way, hiring a babysitter for a few hours totally counts!) You might not believe me, but you will make more money if you make more time for you to do what you do best. At some point, you'll realize it's true. I hope you come to that realization faster than I did.

Automation

This is a critical piece of your support structure, especially when it comes to your marketing. Automated marketing means you have systems set up to continually bring you fresh leads and new clients while you're busy working on other things. It keeps you off that feast-or-famine roller-coaster ride that freelancers dread.

Automation might mean you have a blog that you regularly update. When people like what they read there, they can sign up through a form on your website to get a free report or

20-minute consultation with you. Fresh leads come to you without you having to go out and hunt for them.

Your web form automatically sends them an email to schedule an appointment. When they're ready, they contact you to discuss your availability. If you're swamped, you can just tell them you're not available at the moment, then give your next available time slot or recommend a colleague. (It's always a good idea to have friends you can hand off the extra work to. In return, they'll do the same for you when they can't take on any new work.)

Whether you're looking for new clients at the time or not, you have an automated system to keep people talking with you. They may have a quick job you can do easily. Sweet! You just made some extra cash. Or you might just add them to your database and keep in touch with them occasionally. That way, when you do have an opening, you have a potential new client already warmed up and waiting to talk to you.

When you're first starting out, your support structure might be just your mom or your best friend. That's okay. Every structure begins with a single support. Over time, more beams and joists are added, until there's a stable building that can shelter you whenever you need it.

Realize that sometimes pieces need to be replaced. One rotten beam can cause the whole thing to sag or come tumbling down. Pay attention to your support structure and maintain it regularly. You're going to need it for a long time to come.

Turn Down the Noise in Your Head

We *all* have those voices inside us.

The ones that run circles around our brains chanting, *You're not good enough to do this. You don't deserve it. You haven't worked hard enough. You haven't paid your dues. You're not smart enough. Someone's going to find out you don't know what you're doing, and then you'll* really *be in trouble.*

It's not just you. Everyone I meet has the same noise distracting them from their goals.

We either listen to those voices and stay stuck, even paralyzed, or we try to ignore them, maybe stuffing them down deep inside with positive affirmations or even food, drink, and other addictive substances. Maybe we deny they even exist and just chalk it up to exhaustion.

Here's the thing: the voices are real. They are your subconscious mind trying to keep you safe. Any kind of change is risky, and humans inherently resist any kind of risk. So, the voices crop up. It's their job to maintain the status quo, to keep you exactly where you are. Because chances are pretty good that you have food, shelter, and clothing. Your basic needs are met. But if you take that risk you're thinking about, things could get bad.

The closer we get to a breakthrough…

The closer we get to success…

The closer we get to proving the voices wrong…

…the LOUDER they get!

And it's not always just the voices. Sometimes it's circumstances. Stress levels rise. Finances get out of control. Relationships are strained to the breaking point.

One mentor of mine calls this the "shake-up before the wake-up." When you're trying to make a change, such as starting a freelance business or figuring out a remote-working arrangement, it can seem like life is conspiring against you, actively making your dream feel impossible. Realize that you're probably just a few short steps from breaking through and reaching your desires.

Even if you've defeated the voices before, they will return every time you take a new step, accept a new challenge, or try to improve yourself in some way. They will come back. Sometimes they return with the same old tired routine. Sometimes they get sneaky and show up with a different message.

I tried to ignore the voices for years. My pattern was to silence their messages and the associated feelings, usually with food. It worked to some extent. I could numb out on ice cream and everything would be okay for a little while. What I eventually realized was that overeating was my coping mechanism—it was my way of turning down the noise. For some people, it's drinking. Or shouting. Or becoming addicted to various substances.

Eventually, I learned a new way to turn down the noise. A way to hush the voices and the distracting circumstances so I could concentrate on taking the next steps toward my dreams. It didn't require food, alcohol, or drugs...over-exercising, over-working, or fighting with my family...or depriving myself of anything. After I got good at it, I could turn down the noise in my head in a matter of seconds. No matter how loud it was, and no matter how many times it came back.

Want to learn it?

When the voices start getting loud, and I feel that anxiety tightening in my chest, I know that's the signal to do this exercise. Sometimes I only need this once a week. Sometimes I need it once an hour. It doesn't really matter how many times I need it, because it always works. Every time. And the sooner I can notice the anxiety or fear creeping up, the faster I can turn it down and get on with my work.

TRY THIS EXERCISE

Close your eyes, take a deep breath, and listen to the noise. Instead of ignoring any sounds or trying to silence them, allow them to talk. You might hear them saying things such as...

- You're not smart enough to do that.
- You're not thin enough.
- You're too old.
- You don't have the right degree.
- What if someone finds out you don't really know what you're doing?
- What if you make a fool of yourself?
- Who do you think you are anyway?
- No one's going to read this.
- And even if they do, no one is going to like it.
- What if you get bad reviews?
- What if someone makes a meme about you and posts it all over Facebook?
- What if your family starves because you were too selfish to just keep that job you hated?

- What if you can't pay your bills next month?
- What if your husband leaves you?

Blah, blah, blah...

I used to push those things deep down inside me and try to ignore them. Now, I let them talk briefly. I feel the emotions they bring up. Sometimes they bring me to tears, and that's okay. They need to have their say. They are trying to keep me safe. So, I acknowledge them and say, "Thank you for your counsel."

Then I picture a dial on a wall in front of me.

I take a deep breath in...

And as I exhale with an audible *Shhhhhhhhhh*, I reach out with my hand and turn the dial down.

As I'm doing this, I imagine the volume of the noise decreasing (and consequently, my stress levels lowering).

Depending on how amped up I am, and how loud the noise is, I may have to do this more than once. The first time I might reduce the volume from a 10 to a 7. Then I take a deep breath again, and exhale with a *Shhhhhhhhhh*, while turning down the dial again. Hmm, now it's a 3.

Again. Deep inhale, turn the dial, *Shhhhhhhhhh*...

Eventually, the noise gets so low that it just disappears in a wisp of breath. And all is quiet.

Do you see the difference? Instead of stuffing your fears and emotions deep down inside, you can run through this exercise, which simply acknowledges the noise and releases it. The noise is gone. It's no longer affecting you. And you can get on with your next important step.

Is it going to come back? Sure, it will. Every time you start something that your mind considers a risk, the noise will return. But when you practice this method of turning down the noise, you'll soon find that you notice the volume sooner. You might catch the noise creeping up when it's at a 5 instead of a 10.

Do the exercise until the noise dissipates. The next time, you might catch it at a 3. When you get really good at it, you'll notice as soon as the noise starts building. And you'll be able to dissipate it with one deep breath.

People have been using breath-based exercises to reduce stress for generations. Yoga, qigong, meditation—these are all great tools to help you connect your breath to your body to control the noise. I tried all that, as well as just breathing deeply, to reduce the stress. But it wasn't until I learned the technique of visualizing a dial and physically turning it down that I really made progress in dealing with all the mental clutter that holds me back from reaching the next goal.

You might discover another method, and that's great. Maybe you talk with a close friend who can play devil's advocate. Have them ask you questions like, "What's the worst that could happen?" or "Yeah, you're right. You should just go back to that crappy job you used to have." Sometimes that challenge is enough to quiet the voices. You could even look into a mirror and give yourself a pep talk. Use whatever works for you. Just realize that you're going to have to deal with the stress and uncertainty somehow. There are so many negative repercussions when you use food, alcohol, drugs, anger, or some other escape mechanism.

Find a healthy outlet for your stress. One that works for you. Every time. Once you know how to get out of the paralysis that those voices can cause, nothing can stop you!

Wait a Minute!

Sometimes the voices you hear are actually your intuition speaking, guiding you forward toward your dreams. So, how do you know if the voices are steering you toward what you want or holding you back? I would say the answer is found in how you *feel.*

Check in with your body and your emotions regularly. It's one thing if you're feeling physically sick because you've been working in a toxic environment and the voices are telling you, *Get the hell out of there!* And it's another thing if you're thinking about changing your job and the voices are saying, *Who do you think you are?*

In other words, are the voices causing the stress or trying to help you out of it?

This is so freakin' subtle sometimes. It's why we can stay stuck for so long, sometimes an entire lifetime. We just can't tell whether the voices are helping or hurting. Are they right or wrong? I can't give you the answer. But I can tell you that when you learn to turn down the noise—once the stress dissipates—that's when the true voice of your intuition speaks to you. It might be whispering, afraid to speak up too loudly. So, you have to clear the noise first.

I've noticed that the noise is usually located in my head, and my true voice of intuition comes from my heart or my gut. If you're worried that you can't tell the difference, practice turning down the noise just for fun. Don't make any rash, life-altering decisions as a result of what any of the voices are telling you. Just practice making the distinction between what's noise and what's wisdom. It might take a while, but you will begin to see (and feel) the difference.

Once you think you've got it figured out and you know which voices to trust, test it out with something small. Should you go on that blind date? Should you try that scuba diving class even though you're kind of afraid of the water? Should you take a risk and talk to your boss about assuming a bigger role in the company?

Over time, you'll learn to trust your intuition and realize that it knows what's good for you, if you'll only listen.

Conclusion: Work Happy!

As you may have gathered by now, the biggest problem with working independently from an office, or any other traditional working environment, is that there's *always* more work to do. This is true in a traditional setting, too. But you have regular hours there, and once the clock strikes five, anything unfinished can wait until the next day. At least, that's how 9–5 jobs used to work. These days, people just keep working and working so they can keep their jobs (which is partly why that system is falling apart, I think).

When you're working anywhere, anywhen, the ideal is that you work for a certain amount of time and then you stop. You work Monday through Thursday, and then you take the rest of the week off. Or you work 4 a.m.–noon and then take the rest of the day off.

In reality, it rarely works that way. We have clients to serve and keep happy. There are always more customer emails to address. The website isn't going to develop itself! So, we enslave ourselves to the work. It helps if we love what we do; then at least the demanding hours are pleasurable. But work can become a tyrant.

We want to work. We want to grow. We want to be successful and make more money. And we've been conditioned to think that the only way to make more money is to work harder, put in more hours, and cram in more projects. Sooner or later, you'll take a step back and think, *What the heck am I doing?*

This isn't only reserved for freelancers and entrepreneurs. Even remote employees find there's a never-ending flow of work to be done, and the temptation is always there to keep working until the next milestone is reached.

Freedom. Anywhere, anywhen is all about you choosing your own hours. You choose your working environment. If and when you find that the work has taken over your life and you're not really the one in charge anymore…

Please, for the love of all that's holy, STOP.

Reevaluate what's happening.

How much money do you really need in order to be happy? How much time do you really want to devote to work? If your work is your passion and you're completely happy with your schedule, great! Continue on, my friend. You are amazing.

But if you're not happy, something's wrong. Life is too short to let work rule your every waking moment. Here are several ways you can start to take back control of your life.

Schedule vacations first. Look ahead at the year to come. Then find at least four (or up to eight) weeks to block off. You don't have to go anywhere, if you don't want to. Maybe you just want a week to stay home with your kids during the winter holidays. Maybe you're a sports fan and want to spend two weeks glued to the Olympics. Maybe you want to take a month and travel around Europe. (Yes, you could totally work while you do that. But the point is to take some time *off*.)

When you're first getting started, you might genuinely need to take any job that comes along to ensure sufficient income. But most of us wait much too long to start scheduling our vacations. When you schedule your time off for the whole year, it's easier to stick to your commitments. When a client calls and asks about your availability in August, you can simply say you're on vacation for the second half of the month. It's already planned and on your calendar. But if you wait for a convenient time to take a vacation, chances are you'll never do it.

Don't overbook yourself. Take a look at your responsibilities—to your clients, your boss, whomever. Break the tasks down into the number of hours it takes to do them. Are you scheduling 37 hours' worth of work into a 12-hour period? Just because a task comes easy to you doesn't mean it won't take time to complete. We often dismiss how much time we really need, and rarely add on extra time for things such as servers going down, personal emergencies, or hurricanes blowing through the city. Always build in a cushion of extra time. Take stock of your situation every few months. If you have too many clients, or too much work from one of them, it might be time to raise your rates. After all, you're the boss.

Under-promise and over-deliver. It's common for freelancers or people interviewing for remote work jobs to over-promise just to get the gig. They figure if they can do more work than the next guy for the same price, the client will choose them. But it doesn't usually work that way. The best clients are drawn to your expertise, your style, your energy, your portfolio. Price is important, but it's not the only factor. And if you're talking to a prospective client who is truly price shopping, let them go. If all they care about is how cheaply they can get something done, you really don't want to work with them anyway. Make sure they care about the final product.

So, when you're setting expectations with a client or manager, under-promise. If you know the project will take a week, tell them you can have it to them in 10 days. If you are fine with unlimited revisions on a design project, tell them they get two or three rounds. Then you have room to over-deliver. Get that ten-day project done in four days, and you're a hero! Revise six times because you really want the design to be "just right," and the client will thank you for going the extra mile.

Under-promising and over-delivering are not about lying or tricking people. They're about setting reasonable expectations. Clients like to think they are the only people you're working for. Sometimes you'll have to remind them that you're also completing projects for three other people. That's why you schedule things into your calendar, so you know when you'll have time to accommodate them.

If they complain, you can do one of two things. Offer to put them in front of the line for a rush fee. This should be at least 50% more than your regular price. Or you can set up a retainer arrangement. Retainers are a fee they pay to hold your time each month. It means they get priority when they have a project. If a month or two goes by where they didn't have any work for you, the payments still happen. And the hours you would have spent during those two months do NOT get credited to the next month. If they don't use you, too bad. You held the time open for them, so you deserve to be compensated.

Set general working times. While it's true you have the freedom to work anywhere, anywhen, the temptation is always there to work *all* the wheres and *all* the whens. Take a good look at your week and decide when you plan to work. If your best hours are in the morning, set up your day to be finished by noon. If you really want an extended weekend, take Fridays off.

Want to know the secret to not working on Fridays?

Don't work on Fridays.

Seriously. Set your own hours. It's your right and obligation. Don't say, "Oh, if I don't have anything pressing, I'll take Friday off." That's weak. You'll always have something pressing. If your schedule says no work on Fridays, don't work. It's simple…if you let it be simple.

When you do this, a really cool thing happens. You start magically fitting your work into fewer hours. You become more productive. If you know you're closing your computer and heading to the beach at noon, suddenly you'll stop screwing around on Facebook and actually get your work finished.

Work fewer hours. Get more done. It's a beautiful thing.

Set boundaries with your clients. This goes back to setting expectations. Technology today allows people to connect with you 24/7. Clients need to know when they may contact you, how they are allowed to do it, and when to expect an answer. For example, they can email you anytime and you'll get back to them within 24 hours—except on weekends. Or they can text you in an emergency (then define what constitutes an emergency).

Maybe you have a weekly phone call. Maybe you're launching a product and you really do need daily calls, or even hourly check-ins. The frequency of contact doesn't matter, but the expectations *do*. If you don't set boundaries, clients may start texting you at midnight. Or emailing changes for their website and expecting them to be updated within two hours…even if it's your day off. Nope!

Complying with boundaries is partly up to you. If you routinely answer their texts, even if they are not urgent, they will assume it's okay to continue doing so. If you complete every task as soon as you receive it, that will become the expected norm. The more clients you have, the faster that will spin out of control as every client thinks they can get a two-hour turnaround. Set your boundaries and enforce them. Abide by your own rules.

Take sick days and mental health days. When you work as an employee and you get sick, you're expected to stay home and recover. When independent workers get sick, they're expected to suck it up, make some tea, and get on with the work. We don't get sick days…unless we give them to ourselves.

I live in Maine. Much of the springtime is gray and cold and wet and miserable. But every now and then, in April, something magical happens. The sun comes out. The day is unseasonably warm. The birds have returned and are singing. On those days, screw the work! On those days, I wake up and decide I'm taking the day off. I go for a walk in the woods. I head down to the coast to visit my mother. Or I take the kayak out for a paddle. It's glorious!

Every now and then, take the day off. Whether you're sick or you just feel like it. You're the boss. And you can be a tyrant or you can be the "cool boss" who gives everyone the day off now and then. Be the kind of boss you wish you'd had when you were working that crappy job you hated. It's not just a great perk, it will actually rejuvenate you, so you can return to work with fresh energy and motivation.

Surround yourself with things that make you happy. Your environment has a profound effect on your mood and your productivity. That's the whole reason so many people want *out* of their current working situations. That's why people want to work anywhere, anywhen—so they can have more control over their environments. When you're working in an office or cubicle, you're often limited to what photos, plants, or super-hero figures you can use for decoration.

So, when you do gain control over that aspect of your work, time to have some fun! Make your workspace a place you absolutely love. Give it a fresh coat of paint. Fill it with books and art and ceremonial statues, if you like. If you're seeking more space and less clutter, keep this one place simple and clean. Maybe you love fresh flowers—display a new bunch every week, if that makes you happy.

There are so many ways to personalize your environment, even if you work on the couch. How about background music? Just changing the station on Spotify can completely change my mood. Try to appeal to all five senses when sprucing up your environment. What smells make you happy? Could you burn a special scented candle? Or bake a fresh batch of cookies?

Don't settle for generic coffee or tea—it's only a few extra dollars for a beverage that will make you truly happy. What do you want to feel and touch when you're working? During the winters in Maine, I want a warm fire crackling away next to me and a cozy, hand-knit shawl around my shoulders. In the summertime, I want a cool breeze blowing through the window.

Realize that you have the freedom to change your work environment whenever you want. You can work in your home office, or take your computer on the road and visit a new coffee shop. You can rearrange the furniture, change the music, and add new curtains. It's all about being *happy*. When you're happy, you're more productive. Don't let yourself get stuck in a work rut. People commuting to work every day wish they had the kind of freedom you do. So, don't squander your gift. Use it to its fullest advantage in your life!

Be Happy Now

You don't have to wait until you're making a certain income. You don't have to wait for the perfect clients. You don't even have to be working remotely yet. Happiness is a choice, and you get to have it anytime you want. So, why wait?

Success as a remote worker or freelancer is a gradual thing most of the time. When you start out, you might be making less money than when you worked that 9–5 cubicle job. That can be disheartening. But think about why you chose this path. Be proud of yourself for taking those very first baby steps. You are giving yourself an amazing gift—the gift of time.

Time is the only resource in this great big world that we can never get more of. It's the only truly non-renewable resource. So few of us really think about how we choose to spend our time. We work in jobs we hate just to bring home a paycheck. Then, when we get home, we try our best to numb out and forget that we have to turn around and do it all again the next day. We wish away our time as we count down the days until the weekend. Then we try to cram all the fun into 48 hours—again trying to forget that Monday morning is looming on the horizon.

If you're not making the money you want to, or you're a little scared that you won't have enough clients to make it over the long term, step back for a minute. Realize the amazing gift you're giving yourself by choosing to work anywhere, anywhen. You have given yourself the gift of countless more hours in your life. Hours you won't spend on a morning or evening commute. Hours you won't waste in pointless meetings. Hours you won't be twiddling your thumbs waiting on other people, arguing with coworkers, or fighting for vacation time.

Be happy now.

No matter where you are in your career. Be happy now, and you'll never look back!

I wish you the very best of success, no matter what you do or where life takes you.

You can do it!

I believe in you,

Julie

APPENDIX

Employment Emergencies: How to Get Up and Running as Quickly as Possible

Sometimes people find themselves in an "employment emergency." Maybe they were unexpectedly laid off. Maybe they just can't stand their boss one more freakin' day. Maybe they've had an injury and simply can't keep doing their current job. Maybe a regular source of support has run out, and they need to make money *now*.

If you're in a situation like this, let's talk.

You may be a bit shell-shocked right now, and that's okay. It will take time to work through those feelings and circumstances. I'm not a therapist and can't really help you with that part. What I can do is help you to pick yourself up and start making money as quickly as possible. When financial stress is lessened, you'll have more mental bandwidth to deal with all the other stuff going on in your life.

I'm not *promising* that you'll make money with the recommendations in this section. There are simply too many variables, and every personal situation is different. But this is a roadmap for skipping all the time-wasters and non-income-producing activities and getting on with the paychecks. So, no guarantees. But if I had to start from scratch and make money as quickly as possible, this is how I'd do it.

First of all, **take a deep breath**. If you're reading this, you have access to enough money to buy a book. Or you have access to the internet. Or you are able-bodied enough to get to a library. And that's good news. You are probably more loved and supported than you realize. Safety nets, shelters, and charities exist. No matter how helpless you might feel right now, you *will* get through this. Believe that and you're halfway there.

Sometimes losing a stable position is the best thing that could ever happen to you. Parting ways with a bad situation opens the door to something better. The first step is to realize you will get through this temporary circumstance. You have the power to create something *way* better for yourself. Keeping a positive mindset is critical to getting through this emergency as quickly as possible.

Take the following steps one at a time. Don't dillydally. Do what's required and move on to the next step as soon as you can. Speed and momentum are important here.

Take stock of where you are. How much money do you have saved? How long can you afford to live without an income? Where can you start lowering your expenses? Do you really need that gym membership you're not using? Can you downsize your cell phone plan or get rid of cable TV? Can you move in with a friend or family member for a little while?

Make a list of your bare necessities and come up with a number—the amount of money you need to pay your bills and keep food in your belly. You might be surprised how little you actually need to live. But knowing the amount you require is important. Once you get there, you'll be able to breathe a little easier.

Take stock of your skills. What can you do right now to help someone run their business? Can you write? Are you good at graphic design or research? Are you comfortable talking on the phone? Do you enjoy physical labor?

Draft a simple résumé or CV. Don't overthink this. Just write down all your work experience in a nice looking format and get it out there. (There are lots of templates on Microsoft Word.) You don't have to set up a whole website or spend money on business cards. Save that for later. Right now, there are people you can help. Find them and offer your services.

Find people to help. Once you have an idea about what you want to do (and you might have more than one), you need to figure out who hires people for those jobs. Your long-term goal might be getting a permanent remote job at a digital agency, but that can take time. Even if you put your résumé out today, get an interview tomorrow, and are hired on the spot, it can still take weeks before you see money in your bank account. Right now, you need immediate income. So, finding quick one-off jobs through websites such as 99designs.com or Upwork.com will get you started.

Make a list of every place you can think of to get some quick gigs.

Next, go local! Who in your local community might have a need for your skills? Temporary staffing agencies might be a good place to start. Maybe take a walk down Main Street and talk to the shop owners. Could they use some temporary help? You never know.

Don't forget about your past employers. They might be only too happy to hire you as a consultant or on a project-by-project basis. If you're working from home, they don't have to pay overhead costs or benefits. They save money, and you collect an income while working anywhere, anywhen. What about your past employers' competitors? Similar companies in your town? Your past employers' clients?

Start with people you know. They will be easier to contact. Just let them know you're going solo, and ask whether they have any projects you could help with. If they don't, ask them to keep you in mind and put your name out to anyone in their networks who might be able to use your skills.

If you have a good working relationship with someone in a position to hire you on a per-project basis, take that person out to lunch or meet for a coffee. When you're both in a relaxed environment, it can be easier for them to think of ways to help you.

Set up a way to get paid. If you're working with local companies, they'll probably just hand you a check. But if you're getting hired by companies halfway across the country, it might be easier for them to pay you through PayPal, Stripe, Wave, or some other invoicing method. You can use FreshBooks.com free for up to three clients. Start there—free and simple. Then, as you grow, you can get fancier.

Get to work, but don't stop prospecting. It might be tempting to focus exclusively on your first client, and then worry about your next one later. You'll get back on your feet much faster though if you dedicate a certain portion of each day to prospecting. If you're using an online service such as Upwork, answer as many relevant gigs as possible. If you're working locally, ask for referrals. Who else might be able to use your skills?

Work, search, repeat. Spend a certain amount of time working on projects, but also spend some time looking for new work. If you do that every day, you might find you never need to go back to a "real" job. You can get so busy with one-off work that you suddenly realize you're making even more money than before your emergency. Congratulations! You're a freelancer.

No one likes being tossed into the deep end of the unemployment pool. Emergencies can be frightening. But you don't have to turn it into a high-drama situation. Complaining and worrying won't keep the lights on. Getting to work will.

1. Get your mindset straight.
2. Figure out what you can do.
3. Find people who need what you can do.
4. Serve them.

That's all there is to it.

I hope you never need this information. But if you do, realize that you have options. You're going to get through your emergency. And life will get better.

I believe in you.

Julie Anne Eason

References

"Contingent Workforce: Size, Characteristics, Earnings, and Benefits." U.S. Government Accountability Office. April 20, 2015. https://www.gao.gov/products/GAO-15-168R.

D'Souza, Sean. Psychotactics.com. https://www.psychotactics.com/products/chaos-planning-forget-business-planning-and-goal-setting-start-with-chaos-planning/.

Duhigg, Charles. *The Power of Habit: Why We Do What We Do in Life and Business*. Random House, 2012.

"Fifty Years of Looking at Changes in People's Lives." Bureau of Labor Statistics. September 2015. https://www.bls.gov/spotlight/2015/fifty-years-of-looking-at-changes-in-peoples-lives/home.htm.

Hiller, Jacob. The Jump Manual. https://go.jumpmanual.com/a.

Horowitz, Sarah and Fabio Rosati. "53 million Americans are freelancing, new survey finds." FreelancersUnion.com. September 4, 2014. https://blog.freelancersunion.org/2014/09/04/53million/.

Kruse, Kevin. *15 Secrets Successful People Know About Time Management*. The Kruse Group, 2015.

Pomodoro Technique. Wikipedia.com. https://en.wikipedia.org/wiki/Pomodoro_Technique.

"Telecommuting Trend Data." Global Workplace Analytics. GlobalWorkplaceAnalytics.com. https://globalwork-placeanalytics.com/telecommuting-statistics.

"What we tell ourselves with our body language: Amy Cuddy at TEDGlobal 2012." TEDBlog.com. June 28, 2012. https://blog.ted.com/what-we-tell-ourselves-with-our-body-language-amy-cuddy-at-tedglobal-2012/.

Acknowledgments

This book is over 25 years in the making. Working from home is incredible—full of challenges, heartaches, and joys. It hasn't always been easy, but it's always been worth it! I couldn't have done it without the support of so many people, including all my clients and mentors who have taught me so much. I can never truly repay them.

James—Thank you for always believing in me and not complaining when I spent more time with my computer than with you. I love you!

Catherine, Sarah, and Benjamin—Thanks for being such awesome kids! You were the reason I started this crazy career, and you still inspire me to this day.

Julie Willson—Thank you for always having my back and keeping my life so beautifully color-coded and sticky-noted. I couldn't do this without you!

Kevin LeBlanc—Thank you for diving in with both feet and working so hard to give our clients the best possible product. You are amazing.

Tracey Charlebois—Thank you for being my sounding board and support system all these years.

All my beta readers for this book—Thank you for taking the time to give me your feedback. You are all heroes.

Peter Bowerman—Thank you for writing your book *The Well-Fed Writer*. We've never met, but you'll never know how important this book was to me in the early days. I am forever grateful to you.

Damian Boudreaux—Thank you for teaching me that clients can and should be friends for life.

Amy Collins—Thank you for teaching me how to create and sell really great books. Your wisdom and generosity are without limit.

Soumi Goswami—Thank you for always making our books look amazing.

Eled Cernik—Your cover designs are wonderful. Thank you for all your hard work.

About the Author

 Julie Anne Eason is a best-selling author, speaker, and boutique publisher. She started her professional writing career more than 25 years ago covering school board meetings for the local newspaper. She struggled to overcome the typical free-lance feast-or-famine cycle of low-paying jobs and eventually rose to join the top 1% of writers in the US.

She has ghostwritten multimillion-dollar books for thought leaders and influencers in a wide variety of industries. Her first book *The Profitable Business Author*, helps business people write and publish their own books. As CEO of Thanet House Publishing, Julie Anne's passion is helping mission-driven entrepreneurs create books that inspire, educate, and sell.

Learn more about Julie Anne at ThanetHouseBooks.com.

33991408R00126

Made in the USA
Middletown, DE
21 January 2019